RappeRs'
dEliGHts

Rappers' dELiGhts

AFRiCaN-AMeRiCaN COOKiN' With sOUL

BY AL PeReiRa

UNIVERSE

First Published in the United States of America in 1998 by UNIVERSE PUBLISHING
A Division of Rizzoli International Publications, Inc.
300 Park Avenue South, New York NY 10010

Copyright © 1998 Universe
All artists' photography © 1998 Al Pereira
Big Al photograph by Gillian Rogers

All rights reserved. No part of this publication may be reproduced, stored in a retrieval system, or transmitted in any form or by any means, electronic, mechanical, photocopying, recording, or otherwise, without prior consent of the publishers.

98 99 00 01 02/10 9 8 7 6 5 4 3 2 1
Library of Congress Catalog Card Number: 97-62508

Design and typography by Paula Kelly
Printed in Singapore

Acknowledgments (12" remix version):
Strong shout-outs to the folks who turned my idea into this book, especially my editor, Sandra Gilbert and designer, Paula Kelly. Nods also to Charles Miers, Ilaria Fusina, Brigit Binns, and of course, Virginia Lohle and her Star File crew. High-fives To The Queen, LB and Flavor Unit, and anyone who fed me, especially Spinderella and Roxanne. Thanks to everyone who's given rap (and me) a nudge in the right direction: Yo-Yo, MC Lyte, Kid, Jazzy Joyce, Doug E. Fresh, *The Source*, *Vibe*, *Word Up!*, *Right on!*, *Black Beat*, *The Music Paper*, *Spice*, Pretty Special Inc., Charles Rogers, Bill Adler, Havelock Nelson, Michael Gonzales, Yvette Noel-Shure, Tracey Miller, Serena Gallagher, Grace Heck, Anne Kristoff, Taren Mitchell, Ralph McDaniels, Tina Wynn, Anne Donahue, Michael Small, Steven Stancell, Lillie Mikesell and the old Set To Run posse: Leyla Turkhan, Susan Mainzer, Chris Reade, Chris Chambers, Leslie Pitts, Devin Roberson, Aimee Morris, Miguel Baguer, Max Ernst, Charlene English, Ursula Smith, and Jasmine Vega.

Personal kudos to the Big Al and Farrell families, partner-in-crime David Drapkin, Ray, Henry O, Doug Miller, Ken Ilchuk, Frank Ramos and my friends at The Jets, Laura, Lisa, Darrell, Bill, Gerri, Joe, Jane, Martha and the Ehrenfelds, the Friels, The Schiefners, Rich, Jen, The Coach, Donna, Joyce, Don and Maha, KT, and Purrcy, too.

Dedicated to the one I love, my wife, Liz.
Keep cookin' it Old School!

Photos-Front cover: Queen Latifah; Previous spread (top, left to right): Naughty By Nature, UMC's, Ice-T, (middle): Das EFX, Lin Que (Isis), Biz Markie, (bottom): Eazy-E (R.I.P.), EPMD, Kam; Below (left to right): MC Lyte, Flavor-Flav (2), Kid 'N Play (Play and Kid); Inside back cover (top to bottom): Prince Markie Dee, Patra, Tone-Lōc; Back cover: Biz Markie.

QUICK BITES

"I can cook when I'm hungry enough. I can do some mean microwave joints. Me, I can just nuke down."—Biz Markie

"I've got skills in the kitchen. I got a stable base. I check in the crib. I can cook anything, man . . . No small stuff—I can cook technical shit when I need to." —Parrish (EPMD)

"Oh, yeah, I can cook—I've been cookin' for twenty years! You can come out to my place, maybe I'll even do one for you."—Tone-Lōc

"What do I cook? Peanut butter and jelly, greens and cornbread, and ribs. The cornbread's got nothing special in it. The brownies have *something* special in them! Hmm . . ."—Eazy-E (R.I.P.)

"I'm dieting, actually. I've never been on that wild eatin' shit, anyway. It was just somethin' to do. You got to be healthy these days. You can't stay fat the rest of your life. I feel real good, hittin' the weights. Relieves a lot of tension that way."
—Prince Markie Dee (who started out in The Fat Boys)

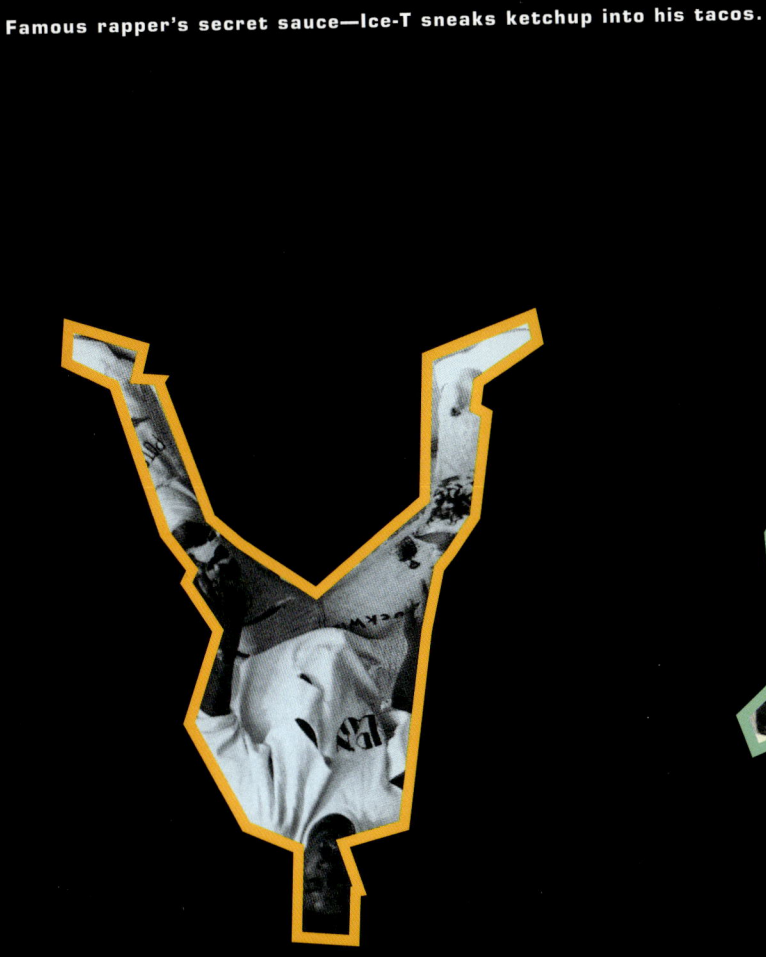

Famous rapper's secret sauce—Ice-T sneaks ketchup into his tacos.

"I catch a frank stand if I'm lucky. You can look at me, I got to remember to eat. My girlfriend will bring me a sizzlin' plate of somethin' while I'm working, and 3 hours later it'll still be there, untouched. You can imagine that doesn't go over so well. About all I can make is a bag of chips open."
—Grandmaster Flash

contents

Foreword by Queen Latifah...8

Intro by Al Pereira...9

1. Eggs, Cheese, + Bread...11

2. Rice, Pasta, + Grains...19

3. Fish + Seafood...37

4. Meat + Poultry...51

5. Vegetables...77

6. Desserts...87

7. Beverages...93

8. Index...96

Photos (clockwise): MC Lyte, Roxanne, DJ Jazzy Joyce, Chubb Rock, Nikki D, Yo-Yo

QUEEN LATIFAH

A WORD FROM THE QUEEN:

I know what you're thinking, "a rap cookbook? But rappers aren't chefs."

You'll see differently after checking out some of the great recipes in this cookbook. I *know* you'll enjoy these recipes. Speaking for myself, I can definitely throw it down in the kitchen, and I'm no chef!

I'm glad to be featured in this book. Cooking is a great form of stress relief, and I try to do it whenever I can. I recently moved across town to a more peaceful place, and I'm back in the kitchen now. I just love good, healthy food, especially when it's prepared by The Queen herself!

So, who says rappers can't be chefs?

—Los Angeles, 1998

WHEN YOU'RE 5'7" AND HAVE A TAG LIKE "BIG AL," there's usually an underlying reason. For me, it lies under the beltline: it's groceries, and lots of 'em. Like me (and probably you, too), many rappers pursue life, liberty, and the perfect wing recipe with equal enthusiasm.

"Cooking is like making music," says Doug E. Fresh. "The same way that you put that snare with this hi-hat and that foot, and you put that voice on top of this one, and combine them and the blend has a certain feeling that's hard to describe. Cooking is the same thing. You might take salt, pepper, oil, potatoes, and onions. These different things together make a different taste."

The idea for this collection came to me as my wife and I were mulling through a mountain of cookbooks and I wondered when someone would write the first rap cookbook. Well, when indeed? How about now. I began asking around and found that, for the most part, hip-hoppers were happy to share their in-kitchen secrets, although slightly puzzled as to why anyone would want to know them. Every time I did an interview or photo shoot, I asked, and these are the recipes I collected.

The same creative spirit that weaves through these artists' music appears in their cooking (well, for the most part). A Tribe Called Quest's "Q-Tip," a studio whiz who can't find his way around the kitchen, admits, "About all I can make is cereal, straight out the box . . . maybe a little toast on the side." Others are no longer able to perfectly express that creativity: KRS-One complains that he can't rightfully procure the main component of his broccoli and cheese dish: "That Welfare cheese was the hypest cheese but I can't get it anywhere now!" There are also those like Luke, who will gladly spill his guts on the various sexual intimacies and wild courtroom brawls that have accompanied his music career but still refuse to divulge the secret spices in his fried chicken: "Nooooo! Can't do that—think of what might happen!" he exclaims. Of course, Luke worked as a professional chef for the better part of a decade.

You get the idea. Owing to the diverse backgrounds of the artists themselves, there is a real mix of culinary treats to be found here. And, while there is no such thing as the vaunted "Cool J Cookies" that LL Cool J waxed angrily about in "I'm Bad," you could do worse than fix yourself a batch of the ones Nikki D suggests (on page 89). Bon appétit, already!

big AL

"I can do the regular, like turkey on the grill, but I ain't no Chef-Boy-Ar-Dee. Eggs. It's simple and that is the way I like to go."—Skoob (Das EFX)

QUiCK
BiTES

"I cook suckers! My mom cooks, my dad cooks. I think I could cook, but the only thing I make is omelets. Cheese and eggs. Benyad throws in two eggs, some chive, maybe a touch of dill, but that's it. I'm not much of a cook.

—Benyad (Blood Of Abraham)

Eggs, cHEEsE, + breAD

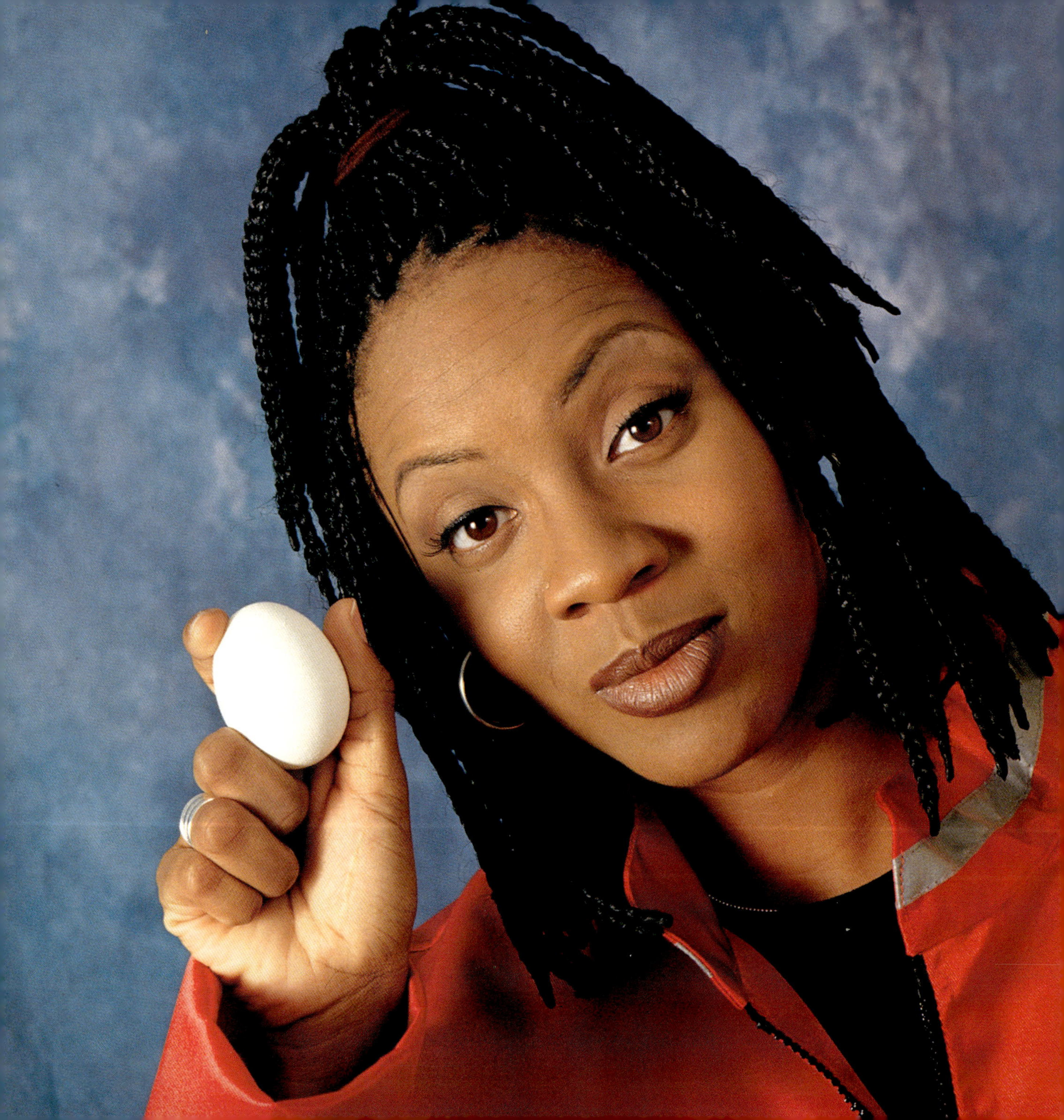

MC LYTE's deVILiSH DEViLed eGGs

THE LYTE ONE MIGHT BE A HEAVYWEIGHT ON A CONCERT STAGE, but in the kitchen, she's still finding her way. She avoids red meat like a bad hair day. A hellion with a mic in her hand, it's not surprising that she likes to prepare eggs with a devilish bent. *"I can make fried chicken—I know how to fry some chicken now! You know what I like? Those Perdue chickens, they are the best. All you do is put it in the oven and wait for that little button to pop up—you don't even have to season it! And I like those, what are they called? Bulls-Eye vegetables. Oh—Bird's Eye! It's gotta be simple for me!"*

"Well, whatcha do is, you boil yourself a couple-a eggs, maybe like half-a-dozen. And, once they're boiled, you crack the shell and you take the egg out. Then you cut the eggs in half, and scoop the yolks outta the eggs and put them in a bowl. An' then you mush it up and then you add a little bit of mayonnaise, an' a little bit of mustard, maybe a cap and a half full of vinegar, and some salt and pepper. Then you mush-a-mush-a-mush-a-mush-a-musha! Then you put it back in the little egg thingys [hollowed-out egg whites] and then you pour on some of that paprika." **serves six**

INGREDIENTS

- 6 large eggs
- 2 tablespoons mayonnaise
- 1 tablespoon French's mustard (or American-style mustard)
- 1 tablespoon white vinegar
- Dash salt
- Dash black pepper
- Dash paprika

rAMpAge's SIMPle sCRAMbled Eggs + ChEEse

RAMPAGE'S MUSIC SPORTS A CHAOS THAT HIS PERSONAL LIFE DOES NOT. "With taking care of my daughter, Gabrielle, I cook, braid hair, wash, I do everything. They call me Mr. Dad. I cook lasagna, I can cook cake, macaroni and cheese, fried chicken, hamburgers, hot dogs, and my daughter loves waffles. Blueberry waffles, I make 'em from scratch. I just put 'em together with flour and everything and I put 'em in the waffle heater, and pop 'em up and she's in the house! Naw, I don't add nothin' to that. I'm not too much on the salt and pepper, tryin' to avoid high blood pressure, we just watch that in my house. Not too much salt; low cholesterol, drink a lot of water. I'm actually trying to work out now, lose a few pounds, so when I get on the road I can be a little lighter on the toes. When I cook, I'm thinking of things like that. Don't want to be tired. I walk a lot, drink a lot of water. Just puttin' it together. The main thing I do is I cook breakfast. Grits, scrambled eggs. I don't eat pork and the only type of bacon I'll eat is turkey bacon. Since it's me, Gabby, and my moms, I use like a half a dozen eggs."

"It's real simple, you just heat up the non-stick skillet, mix the eggs in another place and pour them in, stirring. I like to cover it with a lot of cheese, too. A lot of cheese—fifty-cent worth! Then it's ready when they look cooked. We don't spice 'em much, but you may want to. Serve it with turkey bacon." **serves three**

INGREDIENTS

- 6 large eggs
- 6 slices cheese (American or Swiss)

15

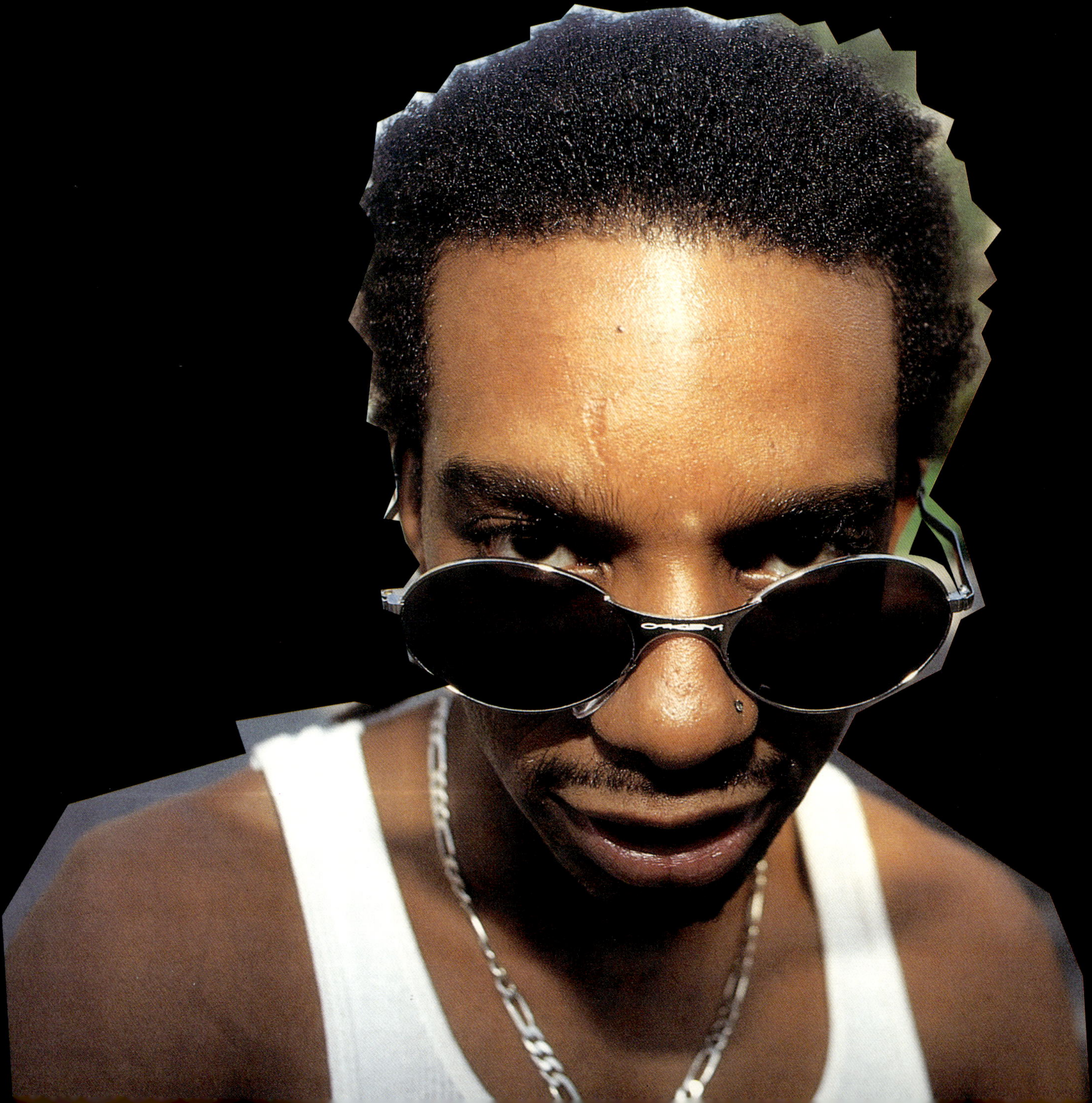

Innersoul's French Kiss Toast

HE MADE A MARK DANCING IN OTHER PEOPLE'S VIDEOS, and Innersoul is out to do likewise with his voice. To date, he's had a less-than-storied career in the food department. But this recipe just might even it up for him. *"I caught a fish recently, but I threw him back in because I felt sorry for him. I can burn a good beef stroganoff. But the best thing I can do is make French toast. I got the dope French toast!"*

"Look, no one puts cinnamon in there, and vanilla extract, and that's my key. If you can get the real extract, cool. Use two or three eggs so that it's nice and thick. Beat the eggs in a dish, adding the vanilla extract and the cinnamon, and run your slices of bread through it, and place them in a heated skillet. Go and get the Challah bread, the French bread, or the Italian bread. Brown on each side. Heat up the syrup and the girls are like, *oh my god!* I kept it goin' a lot of times with that method." **serves two to four**

INGREDIENTS

- 2-3 large eggs
- Dash vanilla extract
- Dash ground cinnamon
- 1 loaf fresh bread, sliced thin (Challah, French, or Italian)
- 2 cups syrup of your choice

QUiCK BiTES

"Do I cook? Nahh. Do I care about food? I'd die if I didn't eat! My favorite dish is spaghetti and meatballs. Can't do it though, man. I tried. I messed up a whole roastin' pan full of that shit. I can't do it, man."—Willie D

"I got kids now so I be doin' my thang, whatever's gonna get done fast. Spaghetti-O's cook fast in the microwave, cuz-o!"—Kool Kim (UMC's, who met his partner, Hass G, while flipping burgers at the Statue of Liberty commissary)

RiCe, pASTa,+ gRainS

Tim Dog's Rabid Red Rice

MANY FOLKS THOUGHT THAT TIM DOG WAS BARKING UP THE WRONG TREE when he called out all of Compton in a battle rap, which sprang the erstwhile Ultramagnetic MC onto the solo path and greater things, though not necessarily in the kitchen. "Yeah, I cook. I cook Southern food, like collard greens, macaroni and cheese, fried chicken, red rice, lasagna, 'talian food. I'm tryin' now to make pastafazoo. As far as makin' red rice, I make yellow rice and basically season it. . . .Y'know, I ain't no motherf—ing chef! I get yellow rice, garlic, cheese, and butter—all that good ole shit! My family is from the South, and one thing my moms taught me is how to prepare a good enough amount to eat. I know how to pick the right amount when I'm gonna eat. That's one thing I learned early!"

"Prepare the rice according to the directions on the package, and then mix everything else in, saving 'a couple-a sprinkles' of the cheese for the topping!" **serves four**

INGREDIENTS

- 2 cups yellow rice
- 1 tablespoon garlic powder
- 1 tablespoon paprika
- 3 tablespoons butter
- 1 tablespoon Parmesan cheese "or a light, mild cheddar"

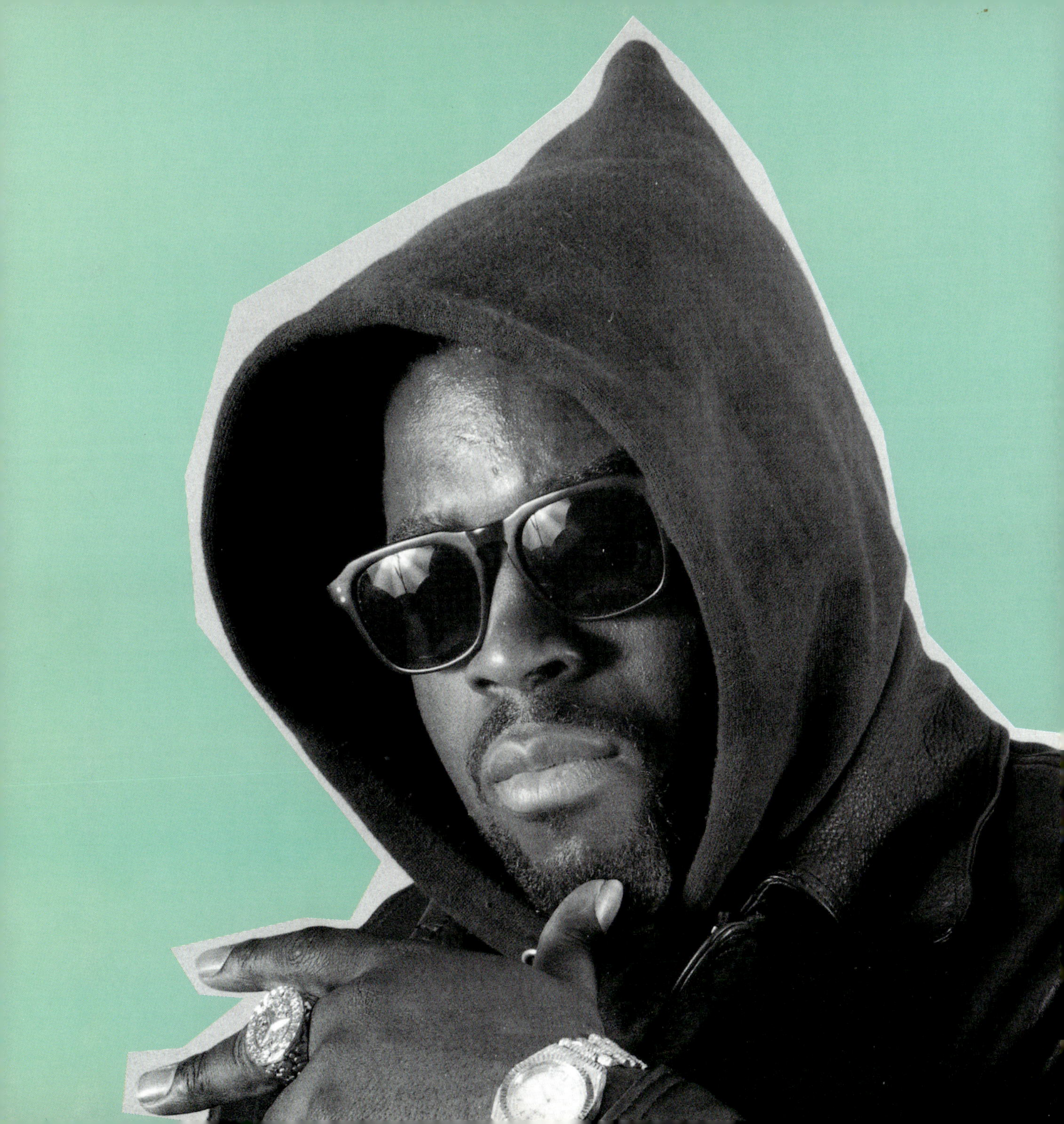

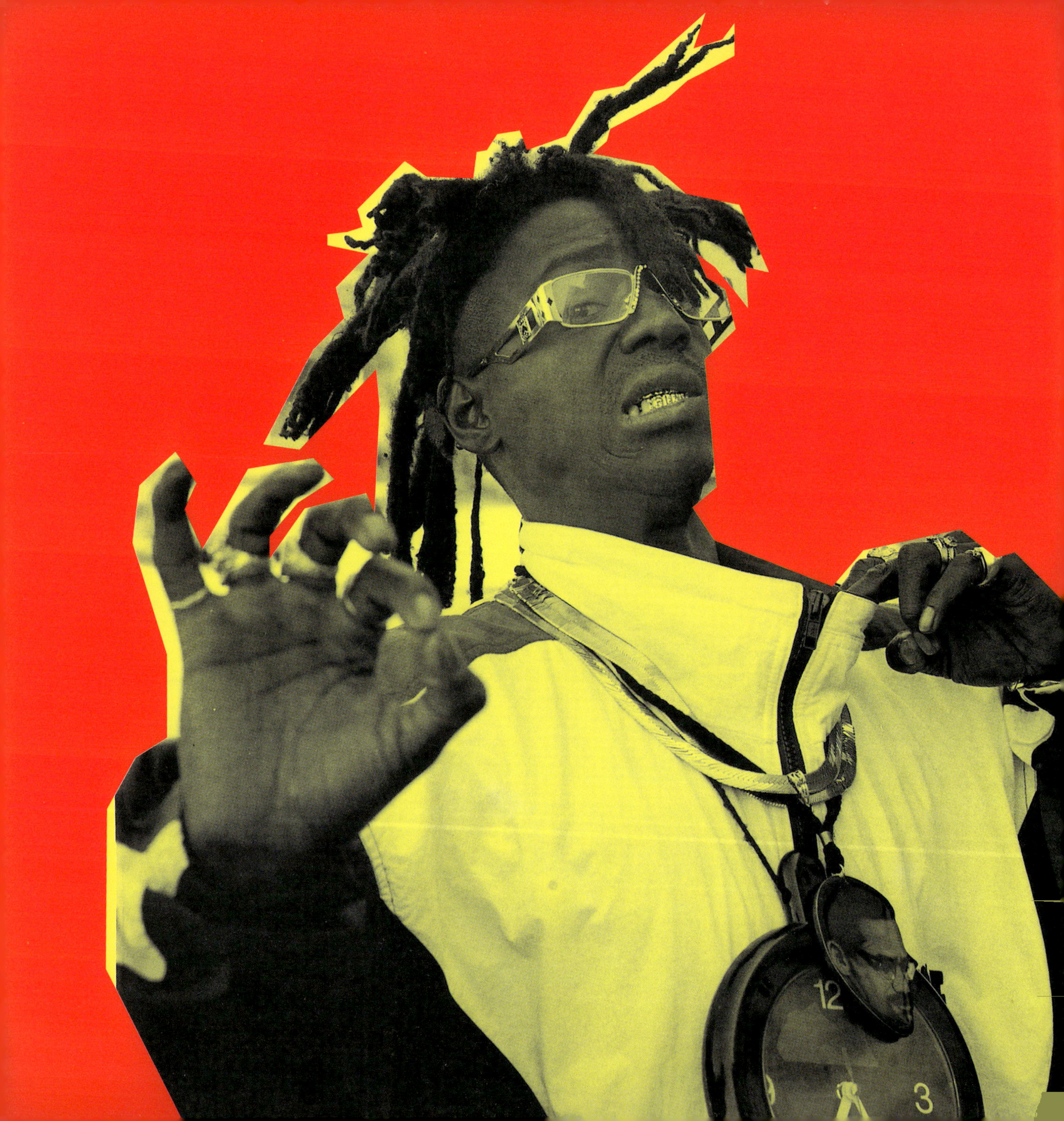

PUBLIC ENEMY'S NUMBER ONE SON is best known as the comic foil to Chuck D and his thought-provoking statements, grinning maniacally and swinging an oversized clock around his breadstick-thin neck all the while. But Flavor-Flav knows the time when the supper bell rings, too. "Sure I cook, man, I'm a chef! Word up, G! I got a chef's degree back in 1977, from Albertson **BOCES** [Long Island vocational training]. I like to cook everything—fettucini alfredo, rice pilaf, crepe suzettes, name it!"

INGREDIENTS

1 **bag of rice**
  + your favorite stuff

"First of all, I go to Carolina, y'know what I'm sayin'—that's where them long-grain-types are grown! Then, after I go to Carolina and get a bag of that rice, y'know what I'm sayin', then I'll take it over to the Jolly Green Giant, because he's got all the vegetables to go with the rice! You mix your peas, your corn, and all of that stuff with your rice and you make it nice! Then you got to take it and you bake it with the beans, and you bake a fine cake for the baby and me! Then it's ready for Flav, I'm tryin' to tell you right now!" **serves six to eight**

Flavor-Flav's Pe Rice Pilaf

jazzy joyce's pasta with shrimp

JAZZY JOYCE IS ONE OF THE TRUEST LINKS back to hip-hop's Old School, and to this day she can set up shop and spin discs with her Boogie Down Bronx ease. But she also has a secret. *"My mom still cooks for me! I'm a spoiled only child—can't you tell? Alright, there's one thing I can make...."*

"First, peel the shrimp and boil, while boiling the water for the pasta separately. Simmer tomato sauce in a saucepan, seasoning to your own tastes. Add the pasta to the boiling water. Drain the shrimp and add it to the sauce, letting it simmer. When your pasta is done to taste, drain and add the hot shrimp and tomato sauce, and toss thoroughly." **serves two**

INGREDIENTS

- ¾ pound shell-on shrimp
- 2 cups tomato sauce, seasoned to taste
- 8 ounces tri-colored pasta, "the spinach adds the flavor"

SPIN'S SPAGHETTIRELLA

WE ALL LOVED THAT "COOKING WITH SALT-'N-PEPA" SKIT way back when on *In Living Color*, and, it turns out, the group did, too. When it comes to spicing up a meal, Spinderella can even make the ordinary spring to life. "I used to cook a lot, but because of all the music stuff, I don't cook that much anymore. My mother cooks a lot for me. I like to make chicken and rice, and lasagna with ground turkey, and my sister makes it with those hot sausages. I don't want to talk about it too much because I'm getting hungry! My spaghetti dish is very fast and easy, and most of all, delicious."

"Place spaghetti in boiling water, enough to cover it. Dice sausages into bite-sized pieces. Sauté sausages in a medium frying pan until tender and juicy, about 10 minutes, on low-to-medium heat. Sauté onion and pepper in a separate pan. Drain sausages and add to vegetables, mixing well. Fold in spaghetti sauce and tabasco. Pour over drained spaghetti. Add Parmesan, if desired. Serve with warm Italian bread, and enjoy." **serves three**

INGREDIENTS

- 8 ounces spaghetti
- 1 pound beef or turkey sausage
- ½ yellow onion, diced
- ½ green pepper, cored, seeded, and diced
- 1 16-ounce jar of spaghetti sauce
- Dash tabasco sauce
- Grated Parmesan cheese (optional)

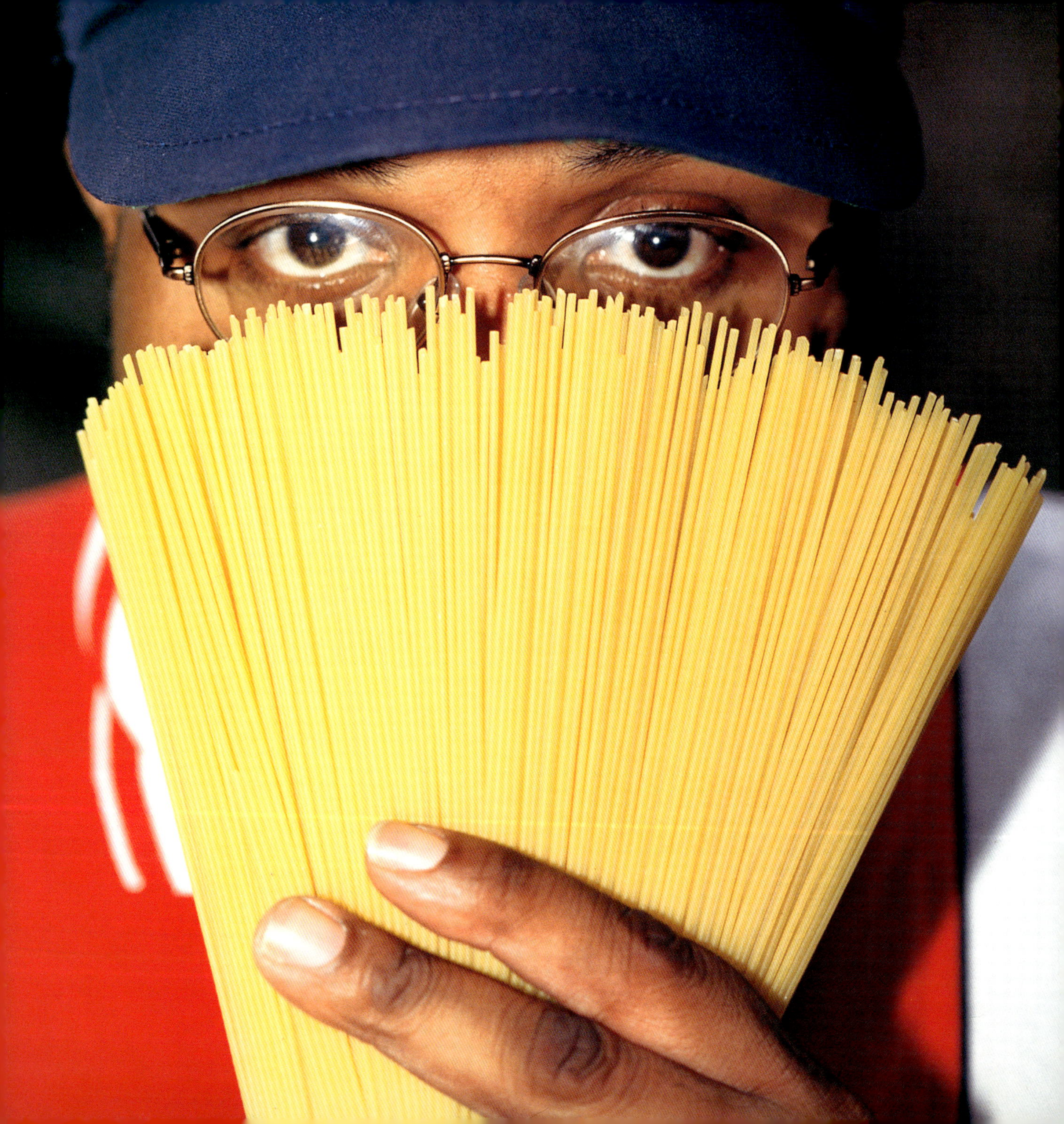

sPaghetti a LA chuBBs

WHEN YOU HEAR CHUBB ROCK glide into one of his trademark deliveries like "Chubb jumped up/The Man, with the plan/Chubb Rock/You know, ah....Judo/A-chop-chop-chop!" it's easy to see how he became a *big man* on rap's campus. Mixing staccato, a Flintstones' reference, and a boast is all in a day's play for Chubbs. What is a little hard to fathom is how he got to be his size without mastering a spatula. *"My mother does big cooking for me most of the time, mostly West Indies food, and my wife cooks, too. I can cook, but I'm no Chef-Boy-Ar-Dee, you know what I'm sayin'? I like to make spaghetti because that's the easiest shit in the world."*

"Boil four quarts water, and throw the salt and spaghetti in. When it's done, you'll know, it'll taste right [follow directions on the package]. Separately, cut up the peppers into small pieces, heat up your sauce in a saucepan, and mix in the ground beef and the peppers. When the spaghetti is ready, drain it, mix it all together and you are ready to eat." **serves three**

INGREDIENTS

1	teaspoon salt
4	ounces spaghetti
2	peppers, red or green, cored, and seeded
½	16-ounce jar of spaghetti sauce
1	cup ground beef

RESIDENT ALIEN IS A THREE-PIECE RAP OUTFIT trying to scratch their way out from an underwhelming debut album. Prince Paul produced, and the fellows gave a spirited performance, but their Jamaican-flavored exhortations went unnoticed. Still, it's good to know that, while they attempt to sort it all out, they won't go hungry. *"We cook a big dinner every Sunday for after the service,"* **Double B.** says. *"We'd go to the service, come back and eat. Sure, we can cook, but tell everyone that Dragon loves his Aunt Averil's cookin' the best. She's the best cook and her plantains are the only ones to have. But the Resident will eat anywhere."* "Yeah," Double B. agrees. *"The best thing is when we make rice and peas. That's it!"*

"It's real simple," Double B. says. "You half-cook the beans in a saucepan, and while that's going on, you take your coconut and slice it real thin. Mix the beans, thyme, coconut, salt, and pepper in the saucepan, cover and simmer for a long time, the longer the better. When it's all over, the liquid from the beans will be gone, and that's when it's ready." (Serve over cooked rice. In this case, peas are actually beans.) **serves three to four**

rESiDeNt aLieN's RicE, pEas, + CoConUt

INGREDIENTS

- 16 ounces canned kidney beans, with their liquid
- 1 tablespoon thyme
- 1 bar coconut
- 1 teaspoon salt
- 1 teaspoon pepper
- 3 cups cooked rice

Young MC's Vegetable + Pasta Medley

YOUNG MC WILL FOREVER BE REMEMBERED for a slice of rap-pop heaven known as "Bust A Move," but there's much more to Marvin Young than that. For instance, he's got a wonderful self-effacing sense of humor. He jumped back in the game late in 1997 with an album *Return of the 1 Hit Wonder*. Besides that, the kid can cook. After a fashion, anyway. *"I'm on a special diet now, so I'm not really cooking much these days. I decided to get into shape. The fatty foods I used to make, I've cut it way down. Most of the stuff I make now would be disgusting to most people! The only thing I do that I can share is steamed vegetables."*

"First thing I do is chop all the vegetables small—not too small, so that they lose their flavor, but bite-size. Then, I'll either steam or microwave them until they are a consistency that I like—5 to 10 minutes tops—depending on how much running around I'm doing that day. You can tell by how they look and by how hot the pot is. Then, I'll prepare the pasta and just mix 'em together—turkey or chicken, too, if I feel like it. And top it off with a couple of sprinkles of cheese."

serves two

INGREDIENTS

- 1/2 cup broccoli florets
- 1 large carrot
- 1/2 cup string beans
- 8 ounces angel-hair pasta
- 1/4 cup diced, cooked chicken breast (optional)
- 1/4 cup cooked, ground turkey (optional)
- 2 tablespoons grated Parmesan cheese or fat-free mozzarella

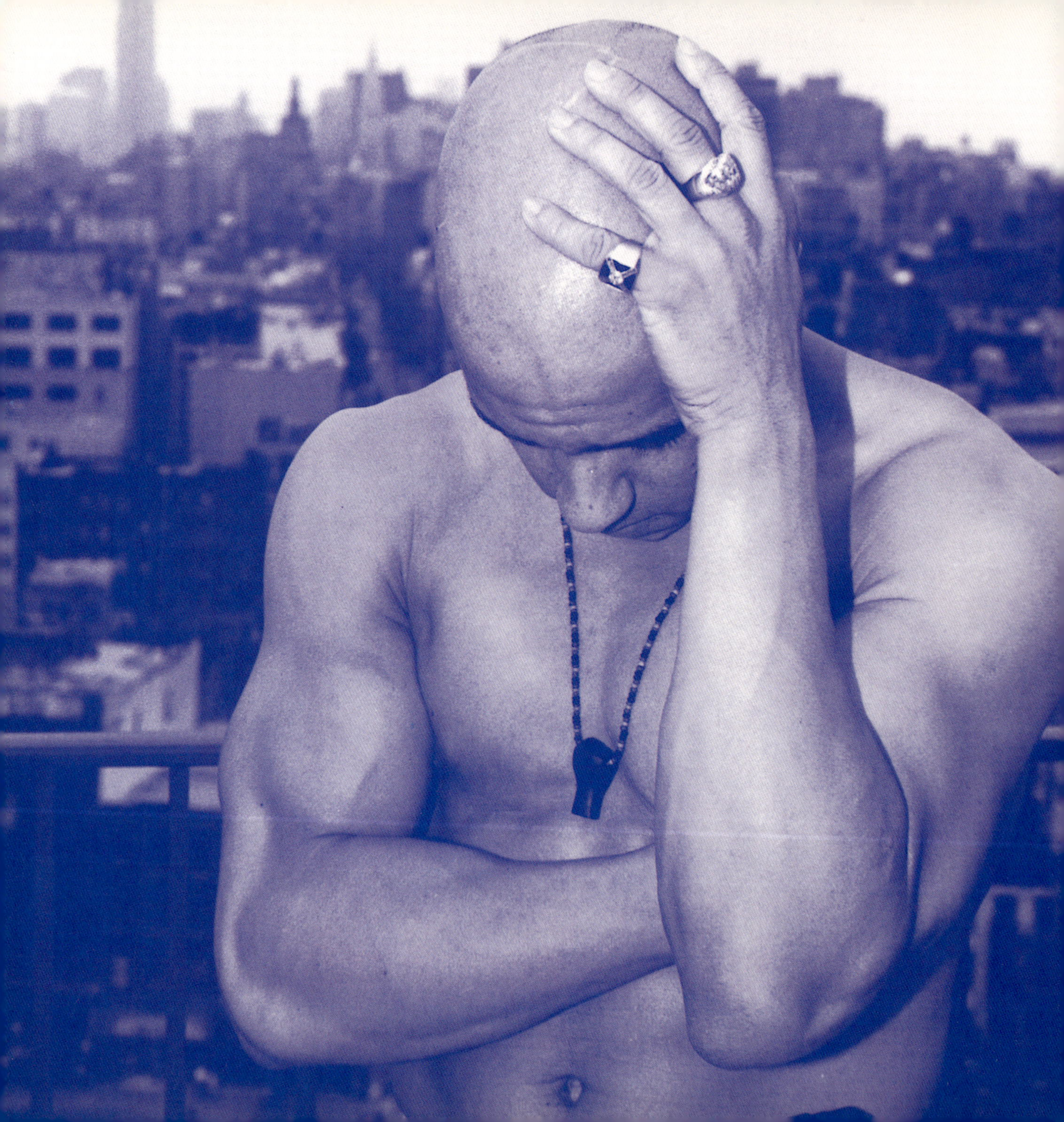

fREEdOM wiLLiaMs' Stir-fRy LaSaGNa

WHILE NOT GENERALLY CONSIDERED A RAP ARTIST, Freedom Williams' hip-hop voice nonetheless resonates nightly around sports arenas with that laid-back mew that he delivered as a member of the C+C Music Factory. The kitchen is no sweat for this diminutive rhymer, either, and he gladly submits this healthy choice for lasagna lovers everywhere.

Preheat the oven to 300°F. "I like to prepare the vegetables first, as a stir-fry, chopped up and sautéed. Then, I mix in like three whole mushrooms, so you know somebody's gettin' a bit of that, and I use the stir-fry in layers, mixed in with the sauce and the egg whites. Take a lasagna pan, put a layer of noodles on the bottom, then sauce, and then I'll take mozzarella and build the layers, and repeat. Cook for 45 minutes, 'cause you really only have to soften the noodles and melt the cheese."

serves six to eight

INGREDIENTS

- 1 eggplant, sliced thin
- 1 green pepper, cored, seeded, and chopped small
- 1 onion, red or white, chopped
- 1 bunch asparagus, tough stems removed
- 3 mushrooms, whole
- 4 cooked egg whites, chopped
- 8 ounces no-boil lasagna noodles, "less messy!"
- 16 ounces tomato sauce
- 16 ounces low-fat mozzarella [about 4 cups grated]

rOxaNNE'S BaKeD ZiTi, bORiQUA-STYLE

ROXANNE BEGAN HER RAP LIFE as "The Real Roxanne," and remains so even with the streamlined handle. *"I love to cook, but it all depends on my mood. I like to make red beans in sauce with yellow rice, maybe yellow rice with black beans mixed in, or chicken cutlets. I'll cook for anyone, except you gotta watch when Chubbs [Chubb Rock] is around, you gotta make him a whole meal on its own or it's all over! You're gonna like this recipe, honey! I love to cook for my girls and my boyfriend, and this is the stuff. Serve with a salad and some bread and you're there."*

Preheat the oven to 400°F. "Cook ziti in a large pot of boiling water with salt and vegetable oil, so the ziti won't stick to each other. Boil ziti 7-1/2 minutes and check to make sure it's not sticky. If it is, cook a little longer. Meanwhile, brown the meat in a large skillet and drain the fat off. Add the next six ingredients, mixing well. Remove from heat. Rinse ziti and combine all of the ingredients except for a little of the cheese. Place in a large rectangular baking pan. Put remaining cheese on top. Cover with foil and cook in the oven for 80 minutes. Remove foil and cook 10 minutes more. Let sit in the oven for 6 minutes after turning the heat off so that the cheese can darken a little, and you are ready for ziti, Boriqua-style."

serves six to eight

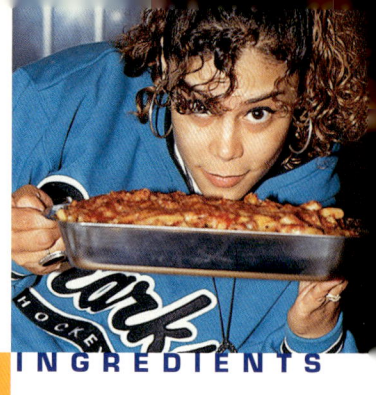

INGREDIENTS

- 16 ounces ziti
- 1 teaspoon salt
- 1 teaspoon vegetable oil
- 16 ounces ground beef
- 1 16-ounce jar of spaghetti sauce, any style
- 1 tablespoon Mom's Sofrito (recipe follows)
- 1 teaspoon Sazon Con Achiote ("or Mrs. Dash Garden Herb Flava")
- 1 16-ounce can plum tomatoes
- ½ teaspoon garlic powder
- ½ teaspoon soy sauce
- 4 cups shredded mozzarella cheese

ROXANNE'S MOM'S SOFRITO

INGREDIENTS

- 2 bay leaves
- 2 green peppers (semi-ripe), cored, seeded, and chopped
- 1 sprig recao (coriander)
- 2 cloves of garlic, minced
- 2 yellow onions, finely chopped
- 3 ajiés dulces (sweet chili peppers), seeded and chopped
- 3 tablespoons vegetable oil

"THE FIRST THING I GOTTA HAVE when I cook is my mom's Sofrito. Us Hispanics all know what's in there—well, not you, Al, but the rest of us! My mom goes and buys everything fresh and makes it in the blender, mixing some [bay] leaves, a few small, round peppers, herbs of choice, and a clove or two of garlic when she feels like it. You can also put the onions and the peppers in the blender, too. You can buy these things at grocery stores such as Associated Food Stores and places where they sell Spanish foods, or my mom'll take you! The amounts vary by how much you need, but it's even. You can freeze it and take it out to use as you need it, using a little spoonful or so each time you cook.

Anyway, chop these things into little pieces, and add a little oil. Put these into the blender and press the "chop" button. You know that "chop" button? And blend them all together. (Add water if needed. The mixture should be smooth but not too watery. Sofrito can be used in any recipe. Add approximately one tablespoon Sofrito to each pound of ingredients.)

INGREDIENTS

4	cups water
	Dash salt
4	ounces American cheese
4	ounces cooked meat, "turkey, ham, or whatever you have left over"
1	cup instant grits

K-ROCK FIRST CAME TO US AS THE STONE-FACED DJ FOR MC LYTE, and is currently pursuing a solo career. He's noteworthy as one of the few rappers who actually gets up early enough to know a breakfast recipe. *"When you come over to my house to eat, you're gonna stay full the whole day. Everyone knows that if they are gonna come over to see me, they're not going to be hungry. My whole family is like that—my sister makes macaroni with yellow cheese and particles of ham in it—that's the stuff! Me, I like to start the day off with a good meal, something that will stick to my ribs the whole day. I've been doin' it for years now, so I know I'm doin' right—you don't need no toast, nothin'. Just remember, you can't put in too much grits or it won't come out."*

"Take a pot and boil water and salt. While the water's heating up, cut up the cheese and meat into very small pieces. When the water boils, add the grits. Return to a boil. Cook that for 5 minutes—a little less if you like your grits gritty, a little more if you like 'em soft. If there's any water left over, drain that and mix in the meat and cheese immediately. That'll stick to your ribs all day." **serves four**

k-rock's breakfast grits

rOSie PereZ's ReALLY rOsiE rEd SAUCE

INGREDIENTS

- ¼ cup olive oil
- 1 clove garlic, finely chopped
- 1 onion, finely chopped
- 1 tablespoon onion powder
- 1 basil leaf
- 1 pinch dried rosemary
- 1 pinch capers, "if I want a different taste"
- 1 16-ounce can plum tomatoes
- 1 6-ounce can tomato paste
- 1 tablespoon garlic powder
- 1 tablespoon fresh or 1 teaspoon dried oregano

THE HIP-HOP WORLD HAS EMBRACED THE FEISTY MS. PEREZ ever since she first slugged her way through the opening credits of *Do The Right Thing* to the tune of Public Enemy's "Fight The Power." She's choreographed the Fly Girls on *In Living Color*, and recently co-produced *Subway Stories* for HBO. "I cook all the time and eat like a pig. I like to cook a lot of Spanish food—that's my forté. But the second thing that I cook really good is Italian food, 'cause I grew up with a lot of Italians. I saw their house and how they eat an' stuff. Like, when you make the sauce, you let it marinate overnight! And you gotta use the peeled tomatoes. I don't use meat. The pasta I like is penne—slightly al dente, not really al dente . . . slightly. And, if I mix anything in, I'll use fish, rock shrimps. The secret is, when the sauce is boiling, you wait 'til the last 2 minutes, throw the shrimp in and only let them cook for 2 minutes. You'll love it!"

"First I put a little virgin olive oil in the pan to slightly sauté the garlic and the onions and the seasoning and stuff. Then put in the whole tomatoes and let that kinda simmer. Then you take the tomato paste (that's what everyone forgets); you need that to add to the thickness. Put that in and mix it up, and let it simmer for a while, and then you add more spices and season to taste. Oh, the key to the whole thing is the basil leaf—you gotta put that basil leaf in there! Yes, one leaf! (But remove it before serving.) And you keep turning and turning. When you taste it, if it tastes a little too acidy or salty, you can put sugar in the sauce. When it all comes nice and thick, take it out and put it in a bowl—a glass bowl, with a lid—and put it in the 'frigerator and let it sit overnight. Then, take it out and cook it up again (reheat to a slow boil) and let all the spices get to know each other. And it's ready."

QUiCK
BiTES

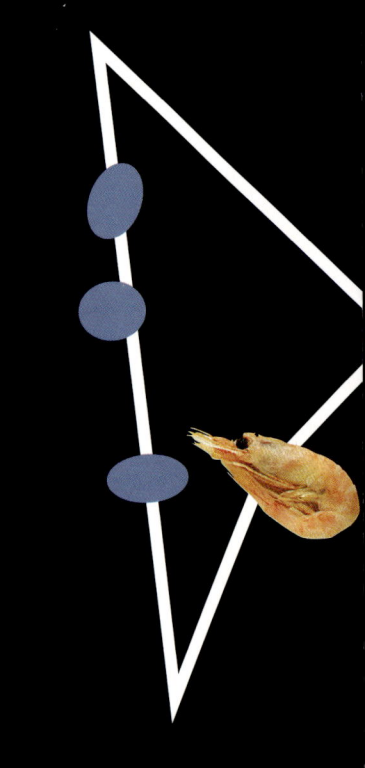

"Yeah, I'm a good cook, that's my main hobby. I like to cook and chill.

I like to cook fish, all kinds of fish. Stewfish, steamfish . . . .

I don't eat meat anymore, for my health. It's health reasons for me—I love my

body and I want to keep it!"—Patra

fiSH + sEaFOOd

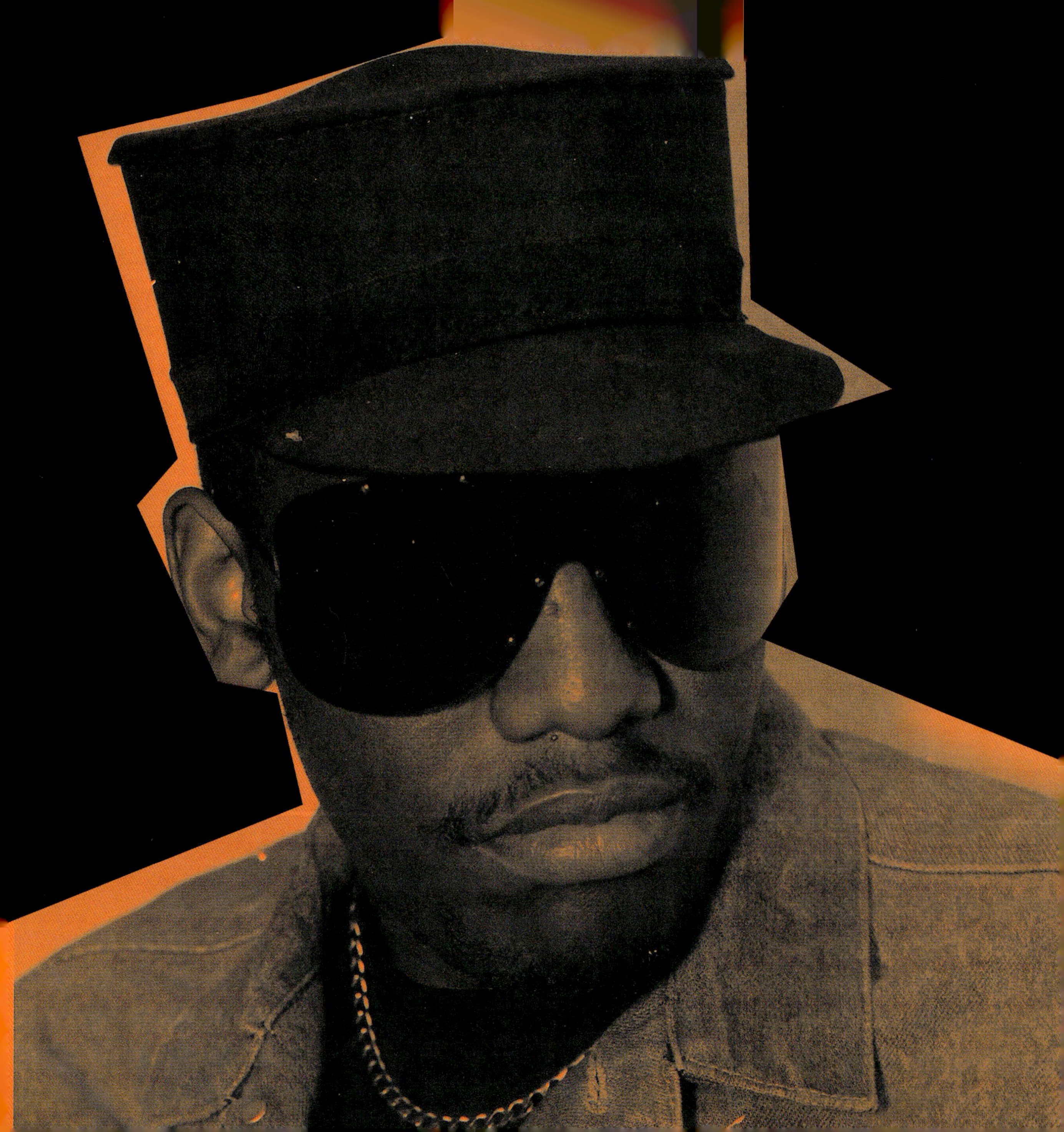

kOOL mOE dEE's sHrIMp sCaMpI

KOOL MOE DEE is one of the longest running shows in rap, and when it comes to cooking, he seems a natural. *"I stay in shape by not eating much. So it's always a real chance whether whatever I cook will come out right. I don't know much about the details of cooking—I mean, what is a 'twist' of lemon? So I kinda play it by ear when I cook, which is why not too many people come to my place when I'm doing it!"*

"After you've cleaned the shrimp, melt the butter in a saucepan over medium heat, blending in the spices. Add the shrimp, and brown them on each side (approximately 2 minutes on each side), and do them to a consistency that you like. Personally, I gotta luck up on it. If I do them too long, they get hard; too short and they're too rubbery. When they look done, they probably are! And that's it. Serve with rice." **serves one**

INGREDIENTS

- 1 cup small shrimp, shelled
- 1 cup butter
- 1 teaspoon salt
- 1 teaspoon black pepper

Ms. Melodie's Sizzlin' Stewfish

THE WORLD FIRST GOT TO KNOW MS. MELODIE when she was both a member of **BDP** and **Mrs. KRS-One**. Both associations have gone south for the Divine Ms. M but, truth be told, these days she's looking a lot more fit and happy. "Thanks for saying I look trim. Think of how I'd look if I worked out! I try to think about what I'm eating—I don't eat any pork. I do a stewfish that's nice, real nice. That's my best meal—just ask my sister, Harmony."

"I heat the butter in a saucepan, then brown the fish in it. Then I remove it, and mix the sauce, onion, pepper, and whatever vegetable goes well with it in the saucepan. Put the fish back in, cover it, and let it simmer for a long time, as long as you can let it [approximately 20 minutes]. Then, serve it with rice."

serves two

INGREDIENTS

- 1 tablespoon butter or oil
- 1 kingfish fillet (about 10 ounces, with skin on)
- 2 cups tomato sauce
- 1 onion, chopped fine
- 1 teaspoon black pepper
- Vegetable of choice

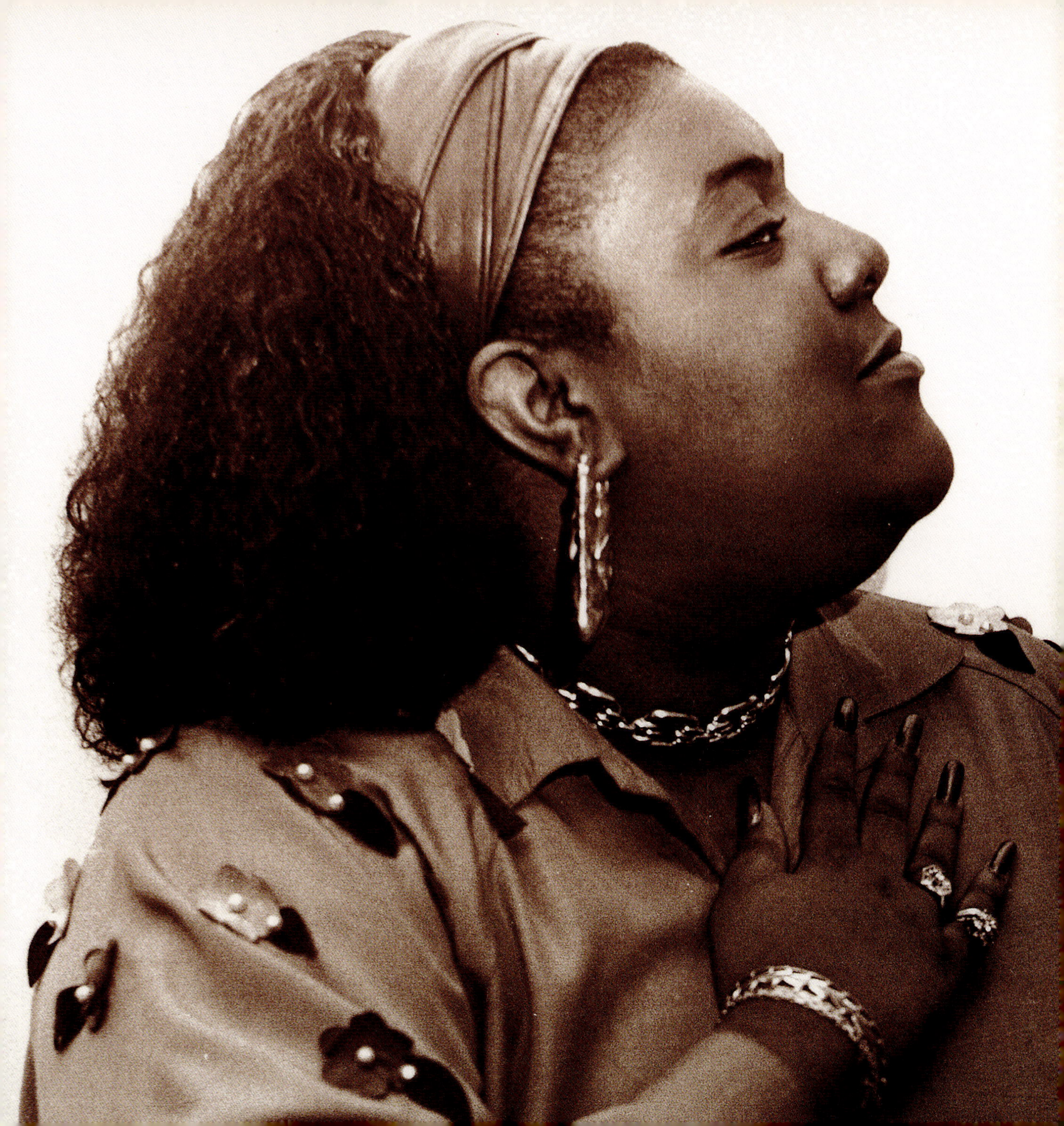

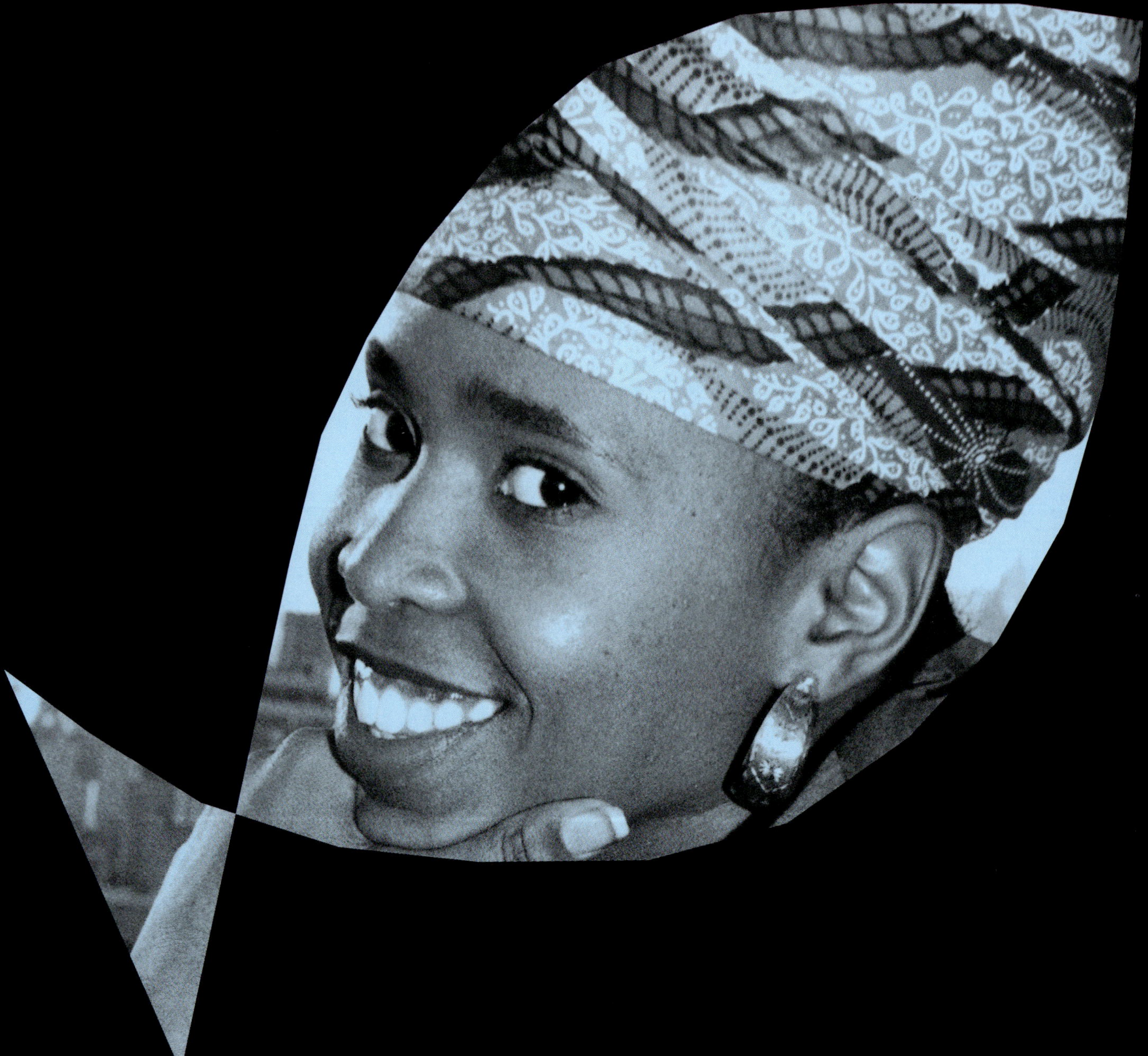

INGREDIENTS

1	bluefish fillet (about 10 ounces)
1	tablespoon rosemary, crumbled
1	tablespoon dried thyme, crumbled
1	cup brown rice
1	head broccoli, tough stalks removed, separated into florets

WHILE HER BIGGEST SOLO HIT to date has been "Pound Cake," nobody will mistake this BDP alum for a cooking whiz. *"I only eat to survive! I can cook a little bit, but I'm not really good at it. I'm not that 'at home' in my kitchen. My sister, Ms. Melodie, she's a real good cook. I don't even know what my best dish would be, but the one that I like to make is bluefish, served with brown rice and broccoli."*

Preheat the broiler. "Take the spices and rub them over both sides of the fish, working it in. Place in the broiler for 10 to 15 minutes or until it is done to your liking. In the meantime, prepare the brown rice [follow directions on package] and broccoli [boil water, add broccoli and cook for 7 minutes] separately. Arrange on the plate and serve immediately." **serves two**

haRMONY's bRoiled bLUEfIsh

Ziggy Marley's snApper dELIGhT

ZIGGY MARLEY'S NOT A RAPPER, he doesn't even play one on TV. But he's such a perennial favorite of the crowd, what would it hurt to have him join us here? "Where I come from [Jamaica], we eat a lot of beans, rice and peas, and fish. So, me and my family, we make snapper."

"Fry the fish first, in a skillet with a little oil, then take the fish out of the skillet and cover it in seasoning. Add water and the rest of the ingredients and the fish to the skillet, and cook it all down for 20 minutes on a low flame, like a brown stew. Cover it so that you can get the steam, and you get the flavor out of the fish." **serves two to three**

INGREDIENTS

- 1 snapper fillet (about 10 ounces)
- 1 teaspoon vegetable oil
- 1 clove garlic, finely chopped
- 1 teaspoon dried thyme, crumbled
- Dash salt
- Dash pepper
- 1 cup water
- ½ head cabbage, cored and chopped small
- 1 carrot, finely chopped
- 1 onion, chopped
- 4 ounces bokchoy, ends trimmed
- 4 ounces calalou greens or spinach leaves

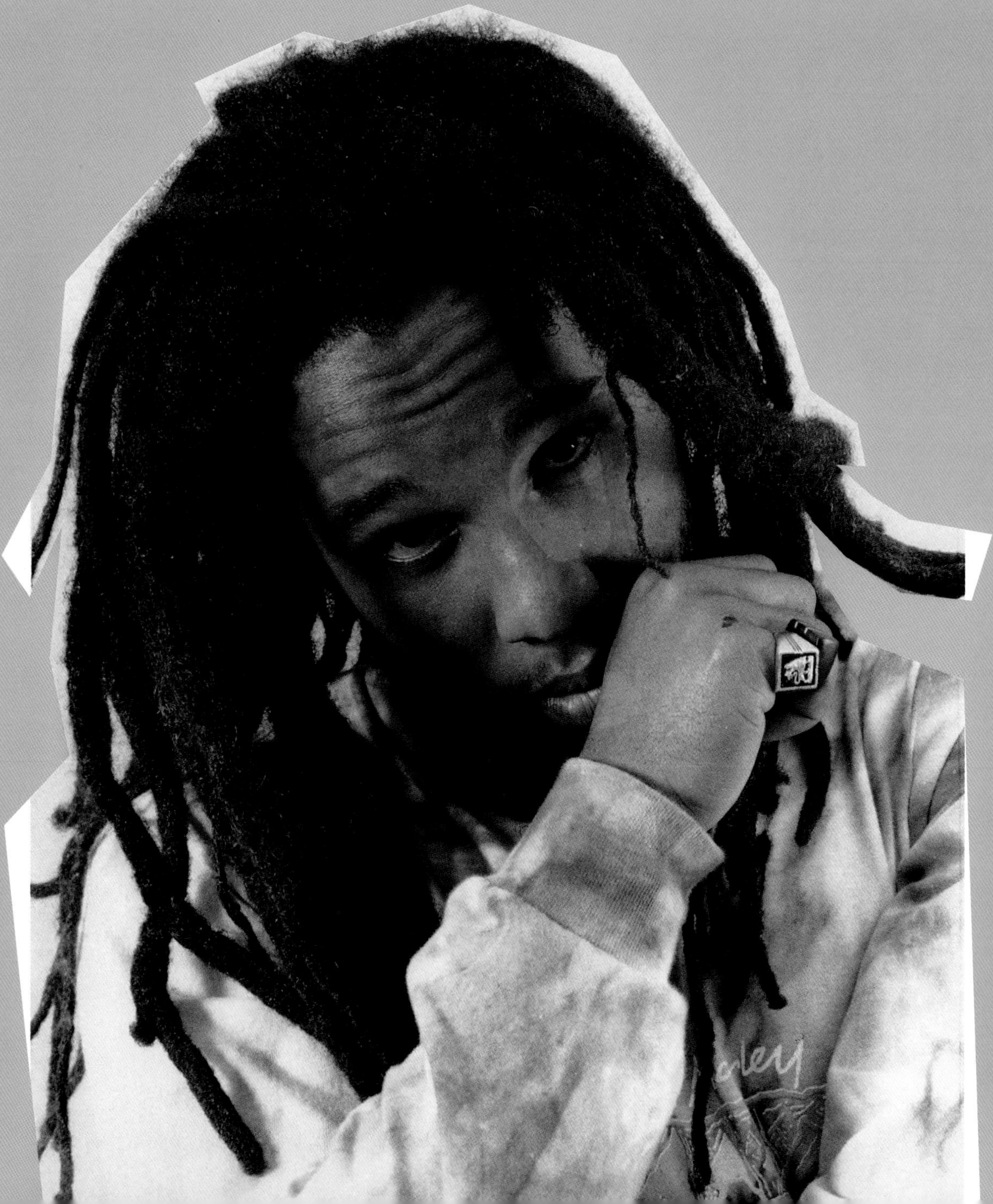

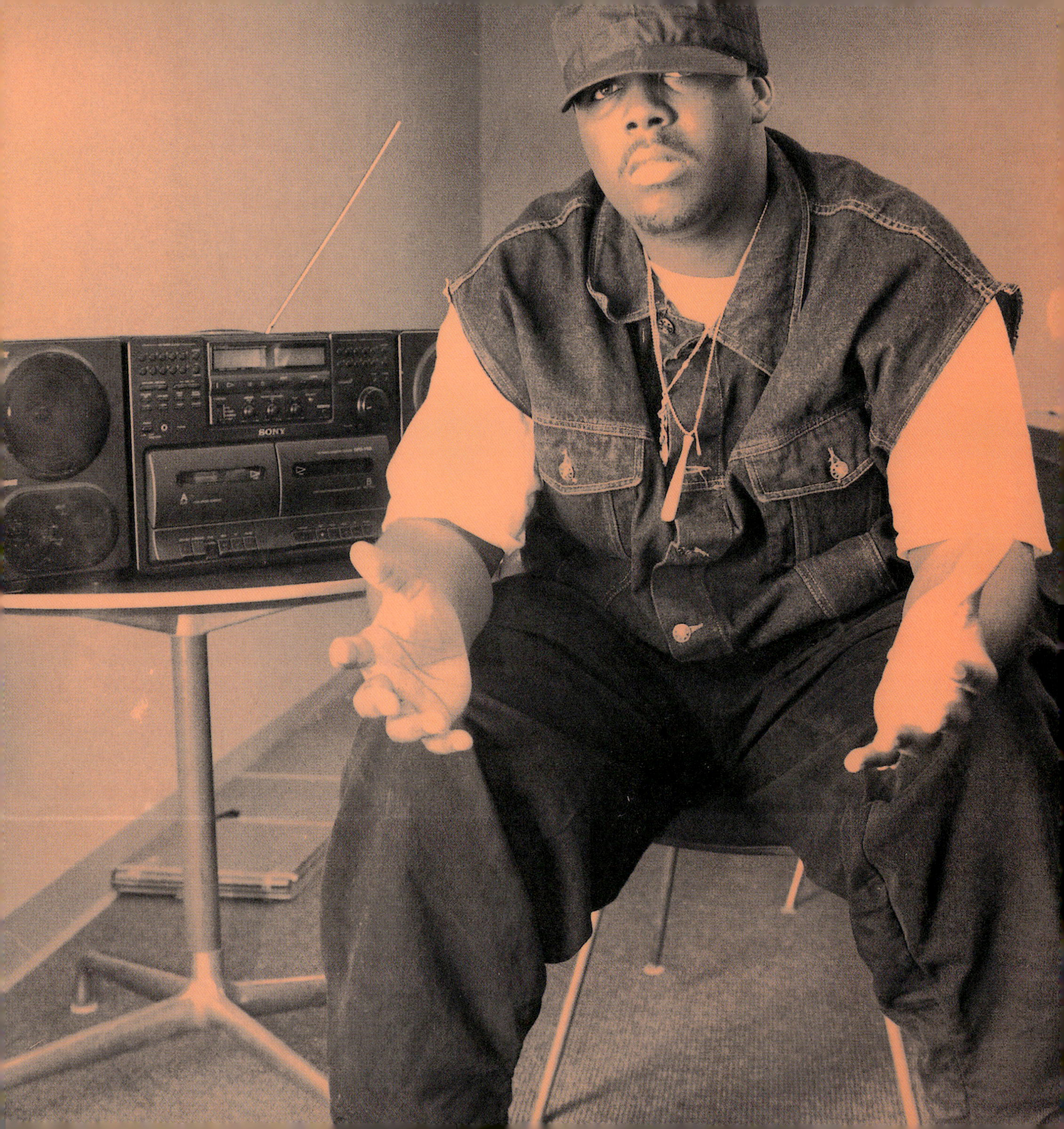
SONY

Erick sErmON's fEttuCini + shrIMp

INGREDIENTS

- 12 extra-large frozen shrimp
- 3 tablespoons butter
- Dash salt
- 1 tablespoon black pepper
- 1 tablespoon all-purpose seafood seasoning
- 1 box Rice-a-Roni fettucini

ERICK SERMON IS THE "E" OF EPMD, as in "Erick and Parrish Making Dollars," a duo successful together and when at odds. He's always comfortable around the stove, though. *"I make this fettucini with shrimp that's real easy— you can make the shrimp taste like the real thing, like they from Red Lobster!"*

"First thing, you take the frozen shrimp out of the bag, open 'em up and run 'em under the water to get the frost off. Then, melt the butter in a deep frying pan and sauté them, put 'em on a low simmer and cover the pan. Then, add your salt and half your pepper and seasoning, a couple of sprinkles until it covers everything. Once it steams and the shrimp start to get soft, take the lid off. It'll be like an oil, that's when you season it and start to sauté. While all of it sautés on a low simmer, boil the fettucini part. This comes with its own spices, so when it's ready, you pour the fettucini in with the shrimps into the sauce—it's incredible! Fix it with Italian bread that you brown for a few minutes in the oven. Incredible!" **serves two**

[You'll notice that there's no Parmesan cheese in here, but Capri invented the recipe, and he'll call it what he will!] **DJ KID CAPRI WAS A LOCAL HERO** in New York until things began breaking his way in late **1991**—first, by hitting the road with Kid 'N Play, and then by becoming the musical director on *Def Comedy Jam*. Now he's a man about town, and a man about the skillet, too.

INGREDIENTS

- 2 tablespoons Crisco vegetable oil
- 16 ounces shrimp (or, "as many as you want!"), shelled and deveined
- 2 cups bottled marinara sauce
- Dash salt
- Dash black pepper
- 1 clove garlic, chopped (or all-purpose seasoning)
- 8 ounces mozzarella cheese

"First, you heat up the oil, then you put your shrimps in, and cook them lightly, so they don't burn. Then, cook the sauce separately, and then add the spices and the shrimp to it. Then let it cook and cook and cook until you just got to eat it. That's the secret, just let it cook. Then, shred the cheese and put it all together. You'll know how much cheese when you break it up and put it on top. Then it's ready—this is the best, you'll love it!" **serves two**

dj kID cAPri's shRiMPs PaRmESaN

mike g's JB Salmon cakes

THE JUNGLE BROTHERS CONTINUE to make their way through the hip-hop jungle with equal parts creativity, reflective thought and a penchant for marching to their own break beat. One of their members, Mike G, has also made his way into the kitchen with style. *"I went to the French Culinary Institute down on Grand Street. During that time, we had finished the album we were working on, so I was sidetracked by a lot of things. I like to mix styles, and I try new stuff. I like French cookin'. What we got from that was basically havin' your organization together in the kitchen, how to have a meal come out on time—have your meat, your vegetable, your side, you want it all to be done at the same time. I like cookin' a little bit of everything—soul food, Jamaican, Spanish—the good stuff! Touré [newest JB member] is my main victim! A soul food recipe I'd pull together would be macaroni and cheese, string beans, fried chicken, and salmon cakes."*

"Get the salmon and mash it up. I like to use flour and water, make a doughy, pancake-like batter almost, and mix in the fish with that, and then add my spices, vegetables. Garlic, cayenne pepper—that's about all I use. Some onions, green peppers, throw it in there. (Form two flat patties). Deep fry them, in maybe a third of a cup of oil. When they are golden brown, they are done. For a side, I would do broccoli and cheese, maybe some rice. Anything, almost." **serves two**

INGREDIENTS

- 8 ounces cooked salmon, boned
- 1⅓ cup all-purpose flour
- Water as needed
- 1 clove garlic, finely chopped
- Dash cayenne pepper
- 1 tablespoon onion, chopped
- 1 tablespoon chopped green pepper
- ⅓ cup vegetable oil

QUICK BITES

"I microwave up a storm. As for Flav, he's lyin' his ass off. He ain't makin' nothin'! What I like to eat? I don't eat beef. Most of my crew is vegetarians, or eat just poultry or fish. Only one who eats anything is Flavor. Anything. Anything.

Aardvark, praying mantis. You see how much salt he put on his shit? You know what I like? Fast foods down South. Chicken fillet. Chicken breast, breaded up. Cool!"—Chuck D

"My favorite thing that I make is barbecued chicken. The recipe that I use originally came from a cookbook that was my father's. I change the spices around a little, but I stick by that. And for the sauce, I use a ready-made one. What do I look like?"—Lin Que (Isis)

mEaT + pOuLtRy

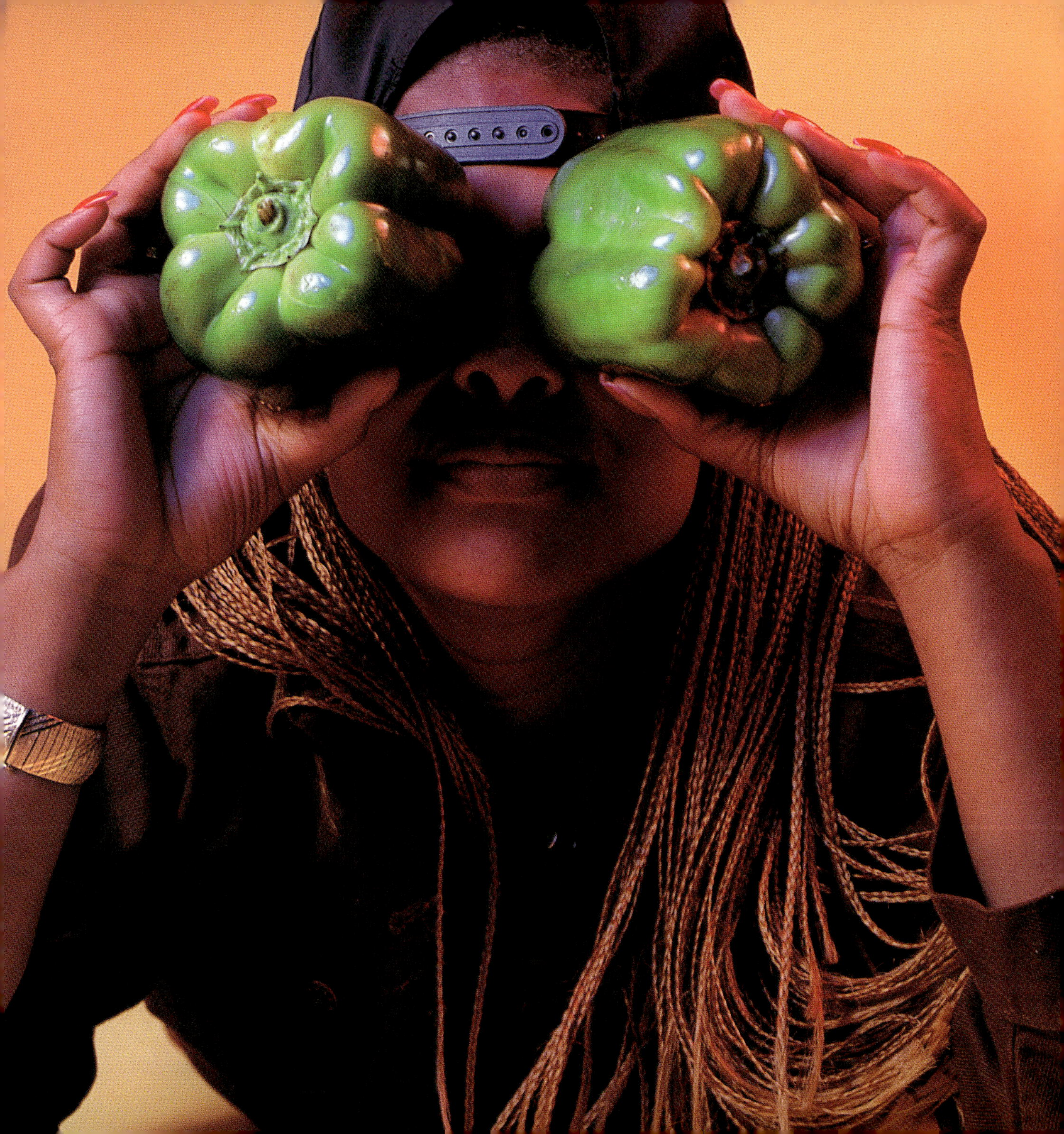

Burritos à la Yo-Yo

YO-YO DOESN'T JUST SPEND HER NIGHTS tearing up stages, she's also got it goin' on in the kitchen where it counts. But don't expect South Central's Black Pearl to kick it with the black beans.

"First thing I do is take my can of beef and mix it with my ground beef, and cook it in a skillet on a low flame. While this is cooking, I cut up my bell peppers and onions into 1/4-inch pieces and add them and let it cook. Drain the fat from the meat, pour my seasoning over it and let it cook some more. When the meat is browned, I remove it from the heat. I then grate my cheese separately. Then I heat up the tortillas on the stovetop, in a clean skillet. Take a tortilla and build about two to three scoops of meat, beans, and rice combined for each, and place them in the shells. Then add the cheese—white, then yellow. Then add a pinch of the cilantro and a drop of sour cream. Roll 'em up and at this point, it's come get your plate! Have it with a nice glass of cherry Kool-Aid, if you don't mind."

serves eight

INGREDIENTS

- 1 can of chunky roast beef, shredded
- 1½ pounds ground beef
- 2 large green bell peppers, cored and seeded
- 2 medium yellow onions
- 1 package taco seasoning
- 8 ounces white cheese
- 8 ounces yellow cheese
- 1 package large flour tortillas
- 1 package rosarita beans, cooked as per label
- 2 cups Uncle Ben's rice, cooked
- 1 teaspoon cilantro
- 8 ounces sour cream

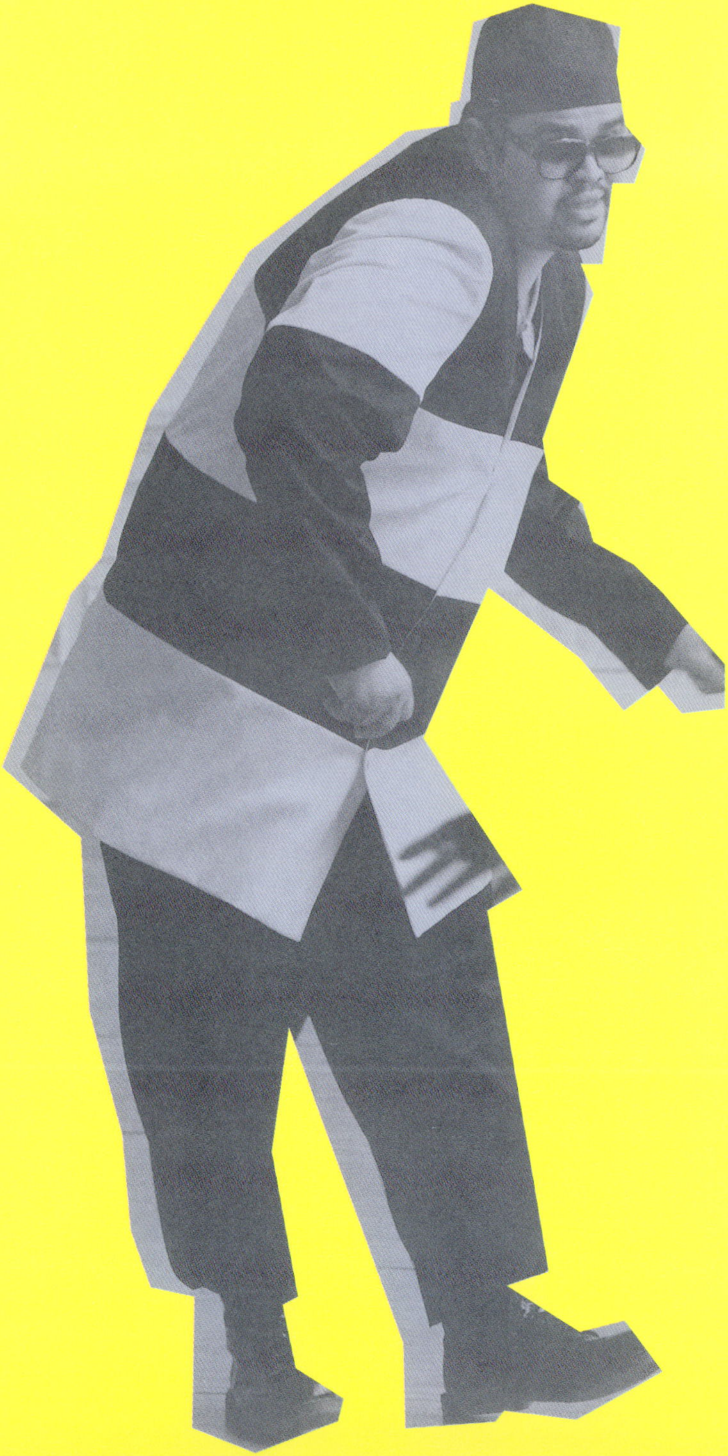

INGREDIENTS

- 2 large, whole bone-in chicken breasts, rinsed and patted dry
- 2 teaspoons seasoning of choice, such as salt, pepper, or lemon pepper
- 2 tablespoons butter
- 1 lemon, halved

THESE DAYS, EVEN THE OVERWEIGHT LOVER IS THINKING OF EATING BETTER. *"My mom, she stopped cookin' a long time ago. She still works, so it's a lot for her. My father likes to cook. For him, it's like a hobby. If my father doesn't want to cook, I'll just get something. When I come home from a long trip, though, it's like they cook for me every night! Every night's a nice meal! I could cook anything—there's nothing to throwing a steak in a broiler. I usually just follow the cookbook, though for me, it's a creative art—once I've made something, I don't feel like eating it. The fun is in making it. I enjoy cooking, too. I'm gonna start doin' it more, 'cause it can be a lot of fun!"*

"Take the chicken breasts and season them how you like them. Heat the butter in a saucepan. Then, fry the breasts in the butter. Take the breasts from the skillet and with a sharp knife, you can butterfly each breast, cutting down the middle and splaying it. Put them back into the butter and brown them until they look ready [until cooked through with no pink remaining]. After that, take a fresh lemon, a *fresh* lemon now, and twist it over the top of the chicken. And you can serve that with fettucini alfredo, done the usual way." **serves two**

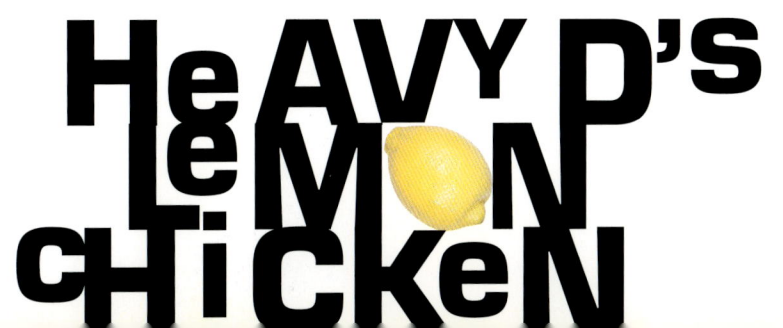

HEAVY D'S LEMON CHICKEN

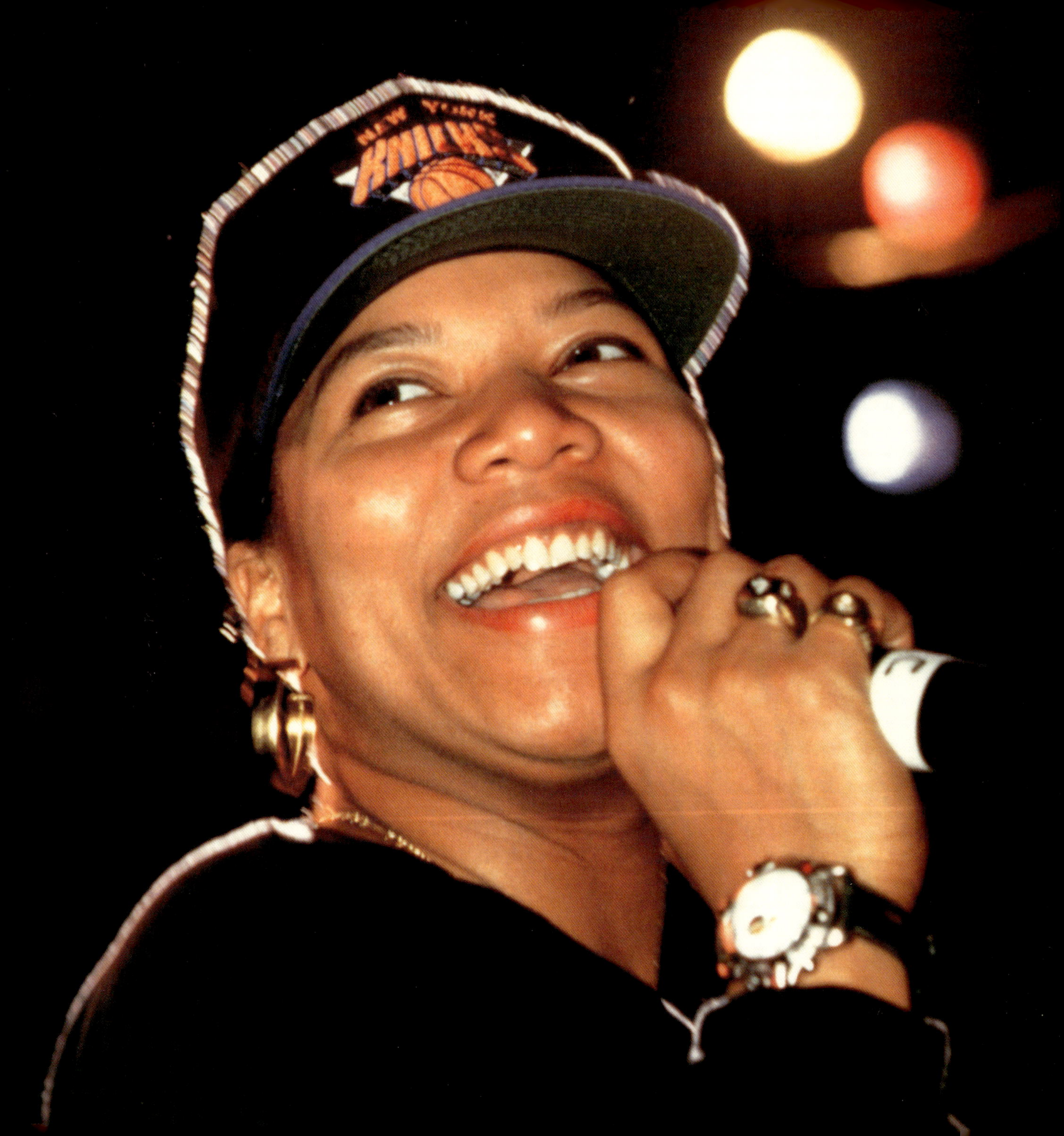
NEW YORK
KNICKS

QUEEN LATIFAH'S ROYAL TURKEY CUTLETS

QUEEN LATIFAH'S RISE IN HIP-HOP and to the top of the mainstream didn't deter her from more pedestrian pursuits. Ahhh, happy is the head that wears the crown.... *"Sure, I can cook. I can do a lot of things well, but the best of these is turkey cutlets."*

"Trim the cutlets. To the eggs, add salt, pepper, seasoning, and a little lemon wine for great flavoring. Bread them [dredge the cutlets in the egg mixture; then in the bread crumbs]. Heat up the butter in a saucepan, and then fry the cutlets on both sides [until cooked through with no trace of pink remaining]. You can serve them with rice or potatoes, whichever starch you feel like, and then add broccoli and cheese on the side. You cook the broccoli [add florets to boiling water and cook 7 minutes, drain] and then sprinkle the cheese over it. The thing I like best is Lipton's seasoned rice, that's right there. This is one great meal that's easy to do!" **serves three to four**

INGREDIENTS

- 1 pound boneless, skinless turkey breast cutlets, rinsed and patted dry
- 2 large eggs, beaten
- 1 teaspoon salt
- 1 teaspoon black pepper
- 1 teaspoon seasoning of choice, such as oregano
- ½ cup white wine, mixed with the juice of ¼ of a lemon
- 4 cups dry bread crumbs
- ½ cup butter
- 1 head broccoli, separated into florets
- 1 cup cheddar cheese, grated
- 1 package Lipton's seasoned rice

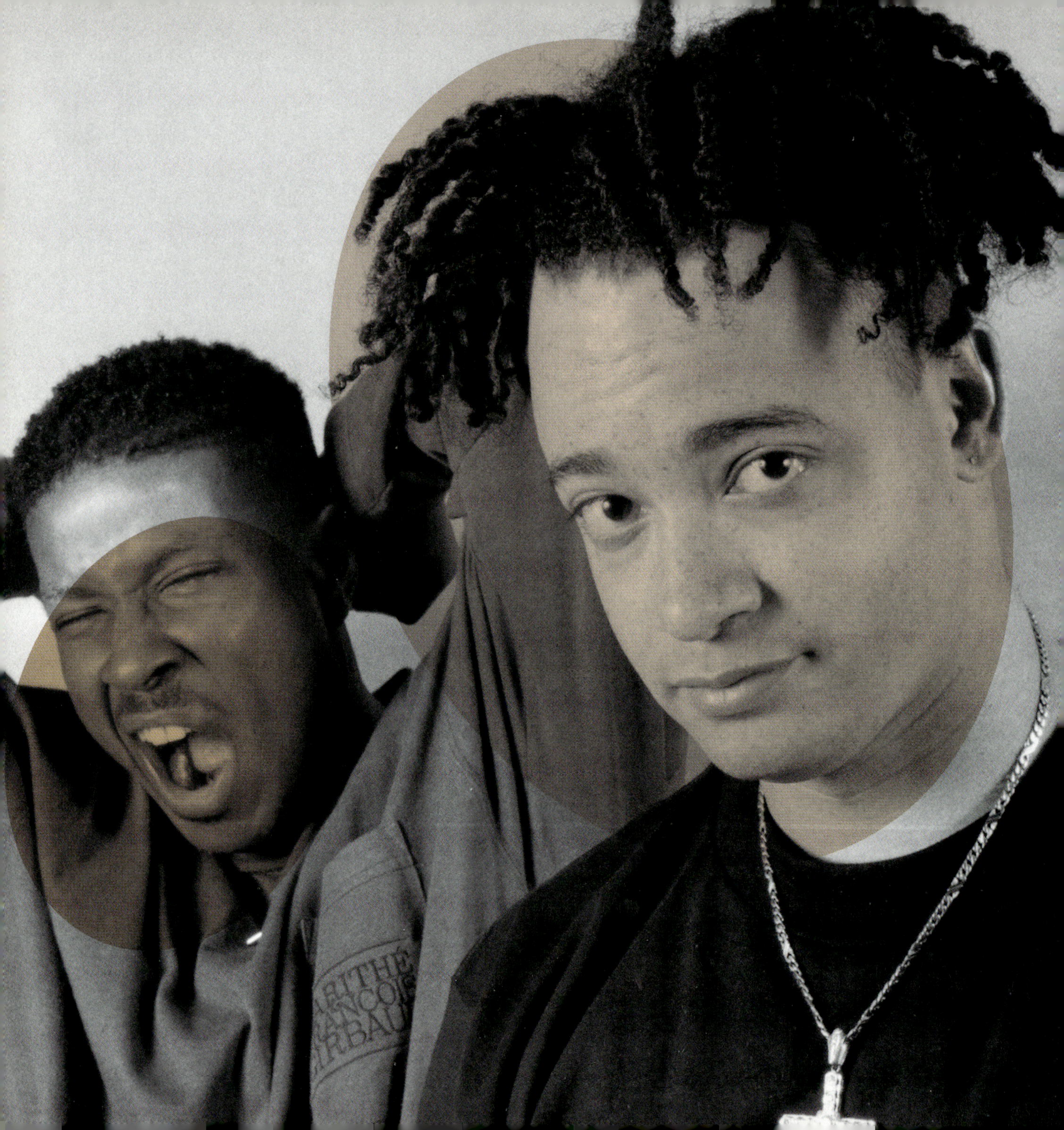

KID 'N PLAY'S HARD LUCK FRANKS 'N BEANS

A CASE COULD BE MADE FOR KID 'N PLAY as the first great crossover hip-hoppers: their success in movies has paved the way for other rappers to take it to the screens, both silver and small. Their high-energy "House Party" series won them legions of fans everywhere, and it comes as little surprise that they attack their food preparation with equal flair. *"We used to make these franks and beans joints when we were mad poor,"* Kid says. *"I was in school and Play had a job, and we lived around the corner from each other. I would call him up and tell him, 'Come over, I got franks!' Though, mostly, he was the guy with the franks. We'd do the recipe with whatever we had in the house. The main thing would be the way that Play would style the meal—it was important 'cause he would set the franks in there and the stylin' was his thing. It would take us through soap operas, make them more meaningful. As a matter of fact, when we go to Wolf's Restaurant for business meetings, Play will still order franks and beans, but they never taste as good as when we would get together and build a meal out of necessity."* **Play concurs,** *"I still dabble: my favorite will always be, 'til the day we die, franks and beans, if I gotta be truthful. That's humble. Humble and quick...and good!"*

"Play always cut our franks lengthwise, he had the whole scenario down. After heating the beans in a saucepan, you make a bed of them on your plate. Then you lay your cooked franks along that, and sprinkle a little sugar over each of the dogs, and you're ready to just chill." **serves two to four**

INGREDIENTS

- 8 cooked hot dogs, cut lengthwise
- 1 16-ounce can baked beans
- 1 tablespoon sugar

THERE'S NO MISTAKING BUSHWICK BILL—he's the only rapper to ignore the "You must be this tall to rap" line. Folks were afraid of him when he first hit with the Geto Boys, but he's a thoughtful soul. And he brings this same insight to his cooking. *"Bein' that I'm an entertainer and I move around so much, I don't always eat right. I always make sure that when I cook, even if I like somethin' spicy, it's somethin' that won't cause a heartburn or any type of upset stomach, or agitate your ulcer or create an ulcer. I like to cook everything—Italian, Jamaican, and American. Since I'm a vegetarian, but not a strict vegetarian, I like to cook chicken parmesan. When it comes to Jamaican food, I like to cook curry chicken, and when it comes to American food, one of my favorites is Buffalo wings. The most important thing with these are soaking them overnight, and using a medium flame. My mom always told me that nothing cooks on a high flame, it only burns. If something cooks, it cooks slow. And the seasonings really need a chance to soak in. This way, everything will be spicy but it won't be overwhelming, know what I'm sayin'?"*

"Dip the wings in the tabasco sauce and let them soak, like overnight. Then, heat up a skillet with the oil, and separate the wings from the tabasco sauce and put 'em in the frying pan, along with the onions and the green peppers and wing sauce. They're done when the wings are firm and cooked [with no trace of pink remaining]."

serves three to four

buSHWicK bILL's bAD-bOY WiNgs

INGREDIENTS

- 24 chicken wings washed and patted dry
- 1 cup tabasco sauce
- 1 tablespoon vegetable oil
- 1 onion, chopped small
- 1 green pepper, seeded, cored, and chopped small
- 1 cup Heinz Buffalo wing sauce (or other Buffalo wing sauce)

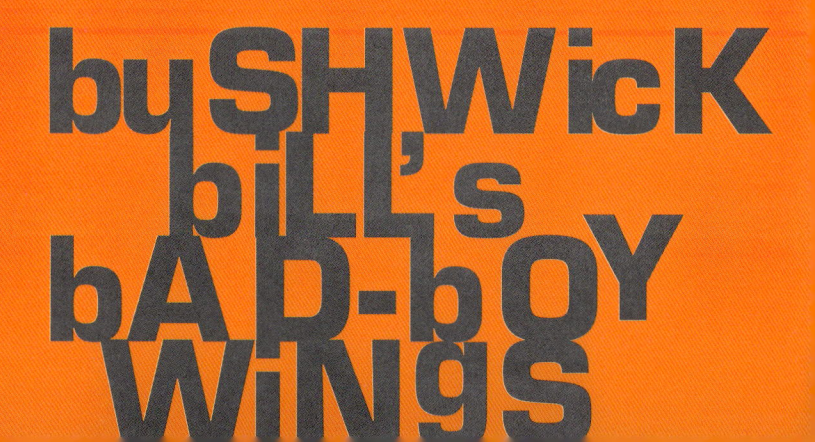

Bushwick Bill in a scene from *Who's The Man.*

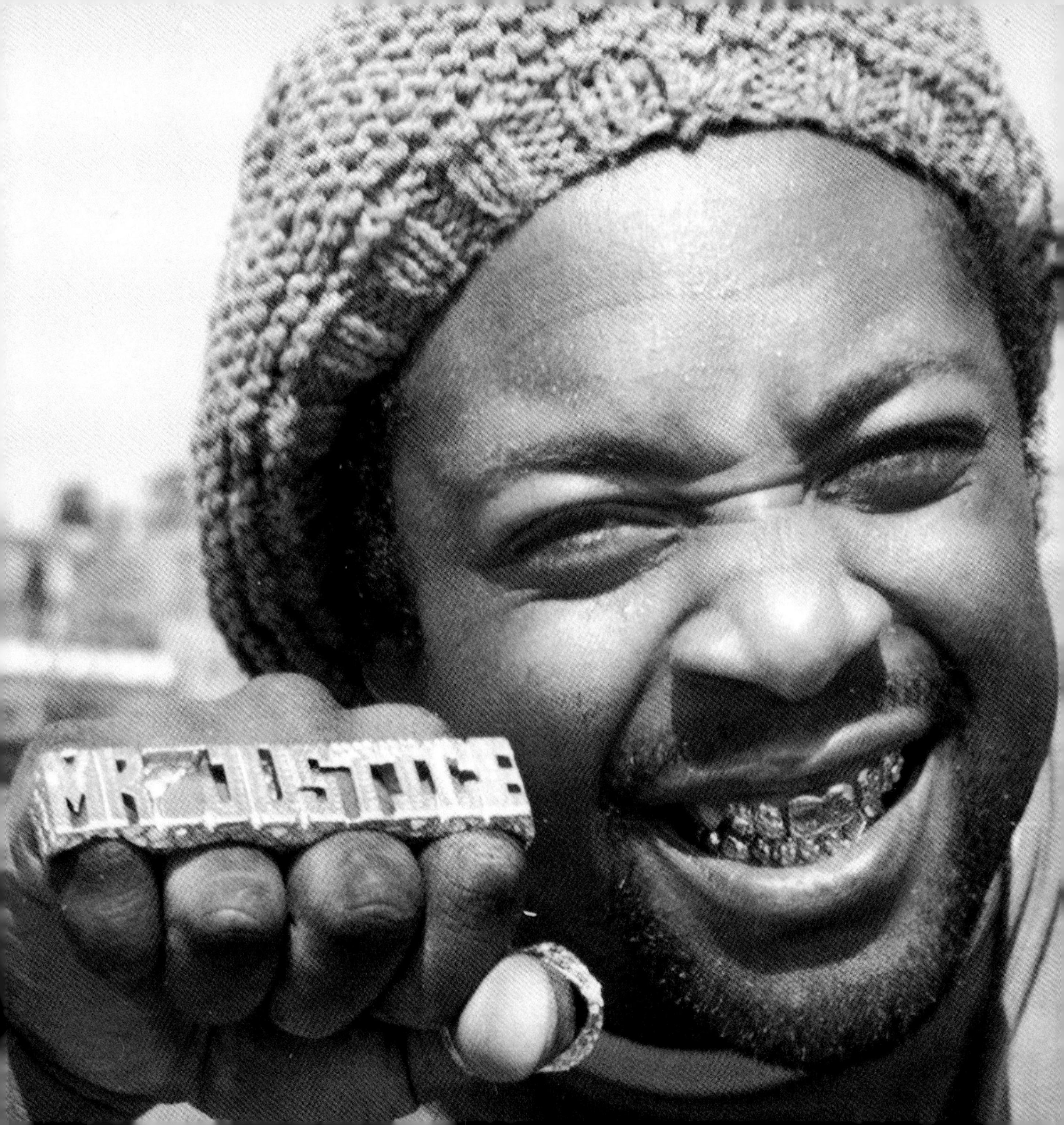

Just-Ice's Hot Curried Goat

JUST-ICE HAS BEEN AROUND since back in the proverbial day, rap's original angry young man. His fury extends to this recipe, a family fave. "My mother's family is from Jamaica, and my father's family is from the South. I don't visit them people—no pork is ever brought into my house. I don't eat no swine. I make food myself, if I want it done right. I make anything I want—curry goat, curry chicken, and jerk chicken. Can we change the subject, man? I gotta go get me somethin' to eat right now!"

"First, you clean and cut the meat into small pieces, pick out the bones. Then cook the meat in a skillet, fry up the meat, stew the meat, and curry the meat well. You add the curry, oregano, pimiento seeds, and garlic powder to the cooking meat and mix it. Throw some dumplings and carrots and shit in there, like that. That should cook on a simmer for about 2 hours, 3 hours, a low heat. That'll come out perfect. What's the matter, you don't cook? You gotta put in those Scotch Bonnet peppers, they're straight from Jamaica—that shit'll burn your asshole out! That's all you need. About two peppers, that's it. Wash your hands real good, and don't touch no other part of your body." **serves four**

INGREDIENTS

- 16 ounces goat (leg)
- 3 tablespoons curry powder, mixed with 1 tablespoon water
- 1 tablespoon oregano
- 1 teaspoon pimiento seeds
- 1 teaspoon garlic powder
- 6 plain dumplings, boiled
- 2 carrots, sliced
- 2 Scotch Bonnet peppers, diced

MaRLeY MArL's fRIEd cHIcKeN

MARLEY MARL'S PRODUCING PROWESS IS LEGENDARY, and he's added his hit-making spin to works by Big Daddy Kane, Biz Markie, and Roxanne Shante. He even resuscitated LL Cool J's career in mid-flight. He built his own studio way up in upstate New York, and the artists still flock to him. Why? *"The typical Marley meal! You'll eat a lot of chicken! When I was in Queens, I used to cook a lot more, but now I mostly order out while I'm working. Of course, I can still fry chicken—I like to fry a whole lot of chicken."*

"Spread the flour out on the table while the oil heats up in a saucepan, on a hot heat. Rub garlic salt and paprika on the chicken, then roll the chicken in the flour. Carefully arrange the pieces in the hot oil and then the best part, watch 'em sizzle! Turn over once and remove when both sides are crispy [chicken should be cooked through with no trace of pink remaining]. Drain and enjoy." **serves two to three**

INGREDIENTS

- 1 cup flour
- 1 cup oil
- 1 teaspoon garlic salt
- 1 teaspoon paprika or red pepper flakes
- 10 chicken wings or drum sticks, rinsed and patted dry

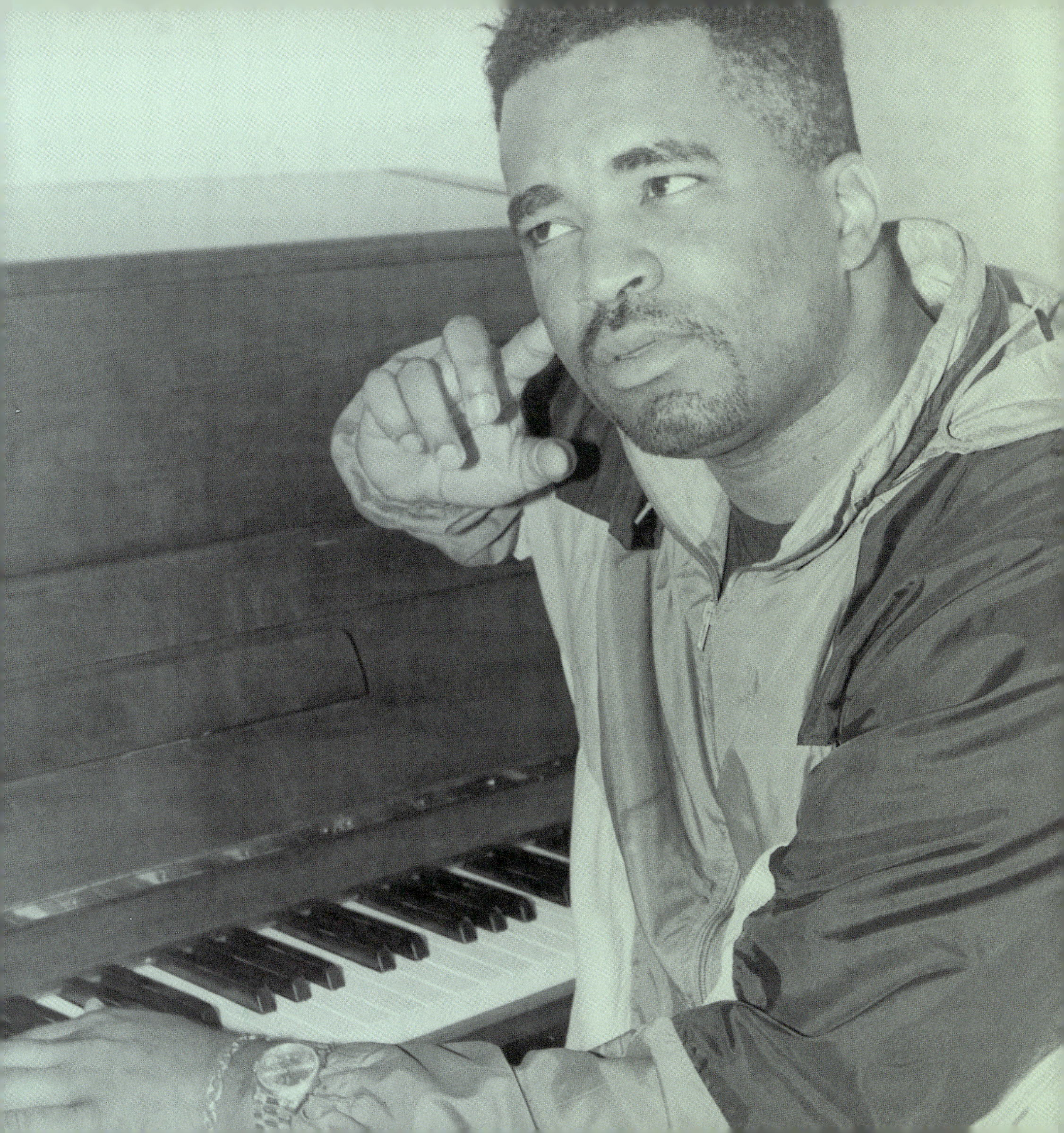

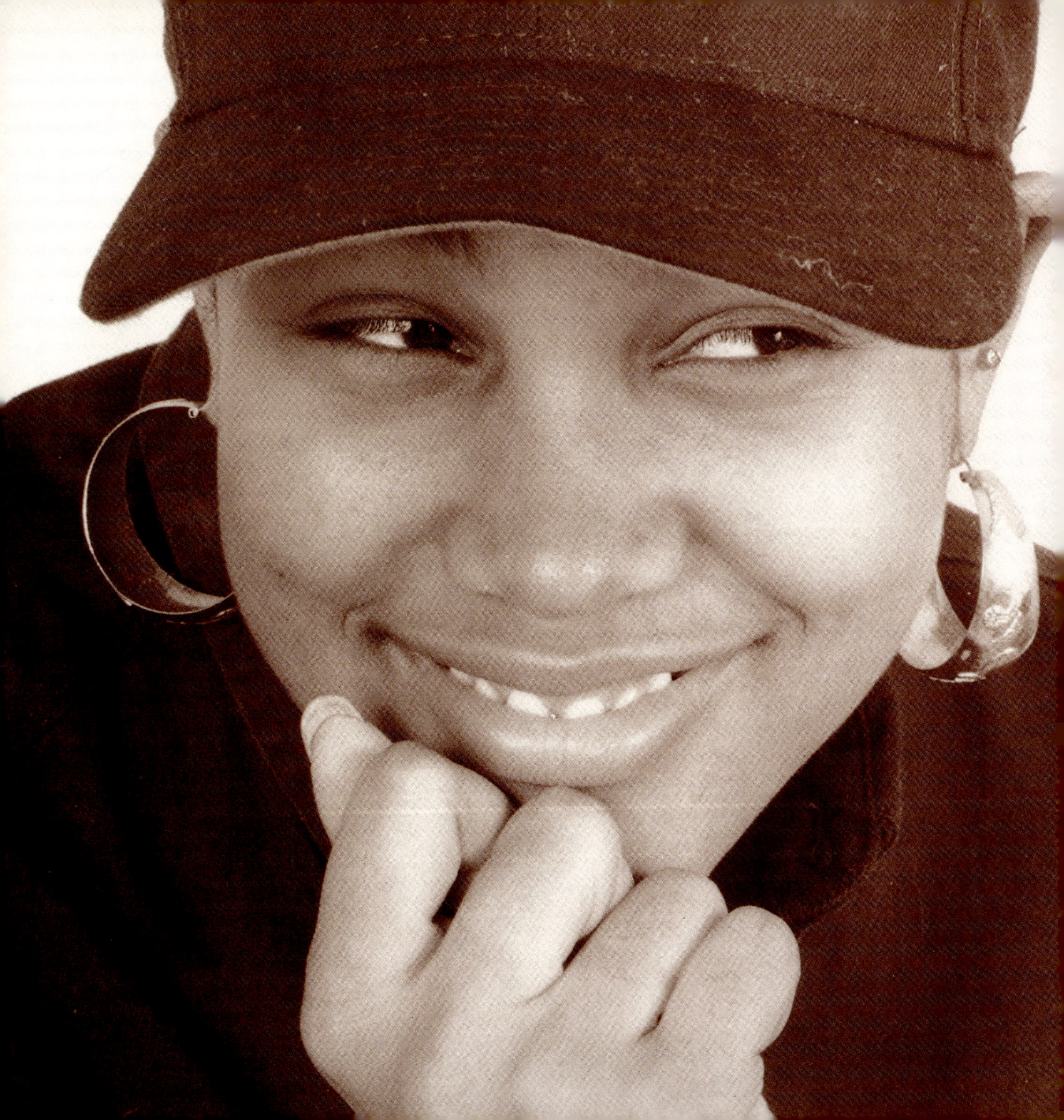

MONIE LOVE'S INCREDIBLE CHICKEN CURRY

INGREDIENTS

- 1 pound boneless, skinless chicken breasts, rinsed and patted dry
- 1 teaspoon salt
- 1 teaspoon pepper
- 1 teaspoon paprika
- 1/4 cup olive oil
- 3 tablespoons mild curry powder
- 1 16-ounce can plum tomatoes, cut into cubes
- 2 tablespoons soy sauce

MONIE LOVE IS ONE OF LIFE'S CHARMERS: if you've got the time, she'll discuss anything under the sun, and a few things above it, too. The diversity of her albums speak volumes, with songs ranging from high school confidentials like "Monie In The Middle" to calls to action like "Born To B.R.E.E.D." But that's nothing compared to her flair in the kitchen, where she puts aside her British underpinnings to cook for her husband and adorable daughter, Charleyna. *"I can cook all of that English cuisine, since that's where I come from, but I do other styles as well. I love to make curries, and after you try this, you will, too."*

"Cut the chicken into cubes. Season with salt, pepper, paprika, and other seasonings if you like. Heat the oil in a saucepan over medium heat. Add chicken to the saucepan and brown. Add the curry powder and chopped tomatoes. Then, add the soy sauce. Depending on your taste preference, add the juice from the tomatoes. Simmer for 45 minutes to an hour, until the sauce is thickened around the chicken. Serve it with rice and vegetables."

serves three to four

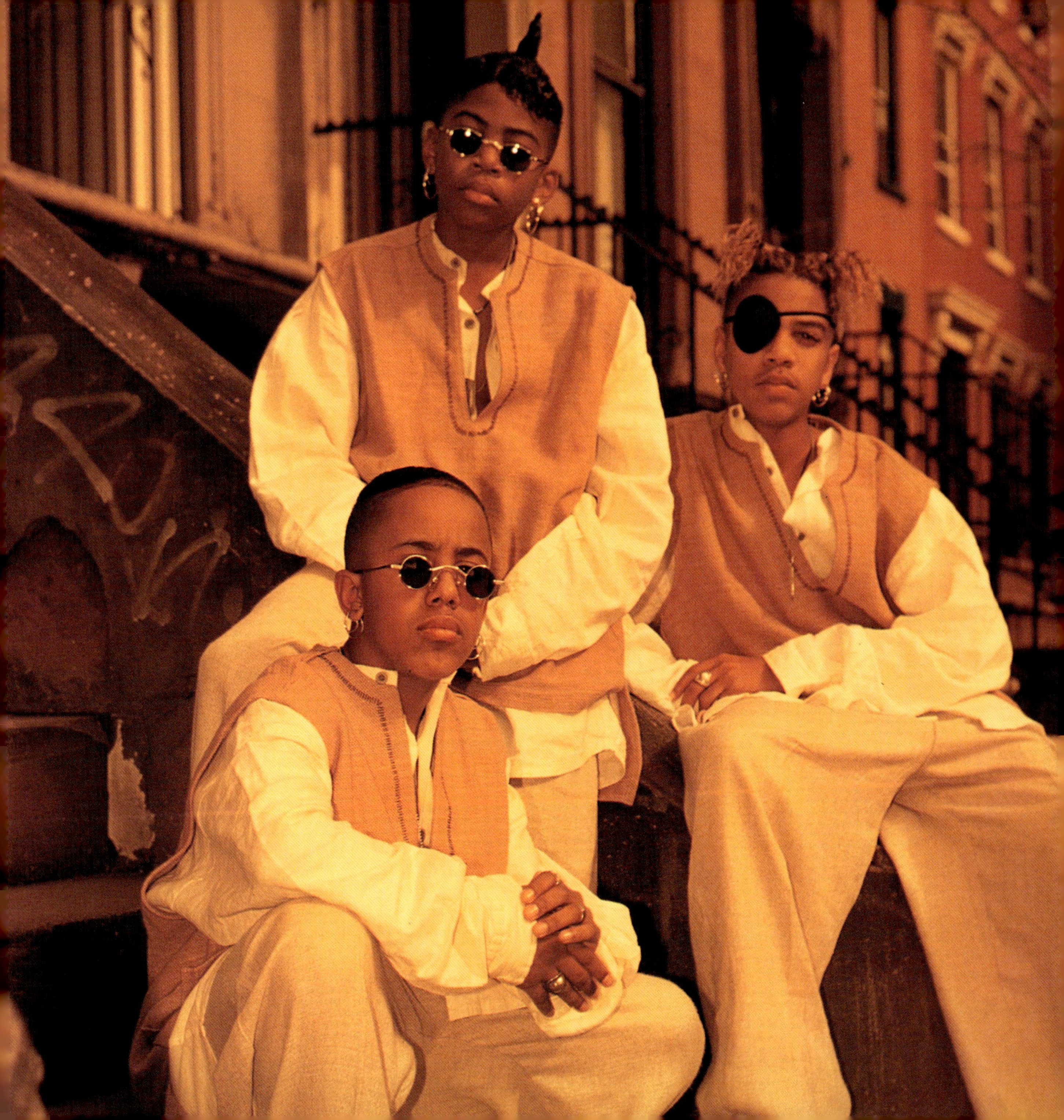

INGREDIENTS

- 2½ pounds boneless chicken breast or thighs, rinsed and patted dry
- 1 cup vegetable oil
- ½ cup soy sauce
- ½ cup sweet-and-sour sauce
- ½ cup mustard

IMMATURE IS THE MIGHTY MIDGET set for the rap world. They carved out an odd space for themselves as moody kids who actually act like kids, and the fans took to them in a big way. Since they are still new to the planet, to say nothing of the kitchen, it's no surprise that they keep it simple. *"We cook, or at least we help our manager cook an' stuff,"* **LDB** *says. "We like to stir-fry, and fondue. To do it by yourself, you need fondue forks, the pot [or a wok], and it's almost like a Chinese dinner. It's like barbecue shrimp, chicken, rice and bread, and baked potatoes, when he's helping us. You make enough for six or seven people and have fun, every once in a while."*

[Cut the chicken into bite-sized pieces.] "It's real simple," bandmate Batman says. "Heat up the oil in a wok until it's hot but not burning. Then, put a piece of chicken on the long fork, and dip the fork into the grease and fry it up in about 30 seconds [until cooked through with no trace of pink remaining]. Then dip it into the sauce of your choice!" **serves six**

iMMATURE'S QUICK CHiCKEN STiR-FRY

TAg TeAM's fRIED pORk chOps, SOUTHe'rn STyLe

"I'VE [DC] BEEN COOKIN' ALL MY LIFE. I learned from my grandmother, my mother, my great auntie, plus I did it on my own. I was just a natural for it. I just did it all the time. I'd just cook things, fry things, mess stuff up, but then they let me get good! All through college, I cooked in restaurants. I cooked everywhere. That was all part of my hustle. I cooked, I sold tapes, I cut hair. My parents had money, but when you're a man, you can't ask your parents for money all the time. You gotta be a man. You do whatever you gotta do to take care of whatever you gotta take care of. Cookin' was one of my things, and I got good at it. I got real good at it! Women love that, that's their favorite thing. Man, if you can cook, you'll have women."

"The pork chops, it's all in the seasoning. It's how you put the batter on the pork chops. I use seasoning salt, pepper, and a little garlic. You can either season 'em light or season 'em hard. Depends on your taste. I like to season 'em hard. Then you throw them in the flour. Turn the oil up high in the skillet, and then you throw them in the oil. But you gotta cover 'em up, so the steam mixes with the flour and it makes your crust. You steam it. The flour turns into a mushy goo. Then, when you flip it over, man, that's when you get the good crust. Just let it sit there in the oil until it's done. Then you take it out and you've got a succulent pork chop." **serves four**

INGREDIENTS
- 4 large pork chops
- 1 teaspoon seasoning salt
- 1 teaspoon black pepper
- ½ clove garlic, chopped
- Flour to cover
- 2 tablespoons vegetable oil

INGREDIENTS

- 16 ounces collard greens
- 8 ounces bacon, thick-cut with the rind
- 1 teaspoon salt
- ½ teaspoon cayenne pepper
- ½ clove garlic, sliced
- ½ onion

ONE OF THE BIGGEST JAMS OF RECENT TIMES was "Whoomp! There It Is," a larger-than-life party record from a pair of large rappers, **DC** and **Steve**, collectively known as **Tag Team**. There's a reason they got that way. *"DC cooks soul food like nobody else,"* his partner says with a laugh. *"He's the soul food king. When he cooks at the crib, after we eat, we have to go to sleep after."* *"Oh, man, I'm the greatest soul food cook,"* **DC** agrees. *"Let's see, what I cook the other night? I cooked turkey wings, slow baked turkey wings, smothered cube steak, fried pork chops (see preceding page), collard greens with bacon, macaroni and cheese, mashed potatoes with **DC**'s secret lumpy gravy, and then, for dessert, just the greatest peach cobbler."*

"First, you gotta wash your greens, then you gotta cut 'em up real good, and then you boil them in water for approximately an hour. Drain 'em. Then, you put some bacon in a pan. You gotta get good bacon, the kind with the rind—Southern-style, black bacon. That's what I call it! Let the bacon fry, and it creates its own oil. Then, you put in a teaspoon of salt, and just a couple of taps of red pepper, and maybe just a couple of slices of real garlic, just enough to make them think: Hey—is this garlic? And that's the flavor, you know what I'm sayin'? Then you cut up half an onion real, real fine. Once the bacon is almost done, you put the onion in with the rest of the seasoning and you flip it about ten times, chef style. Then, after an hour on the greens, you put all of this into the greens, and cook it on low for about 2-1/2 hours. You'll have the most tender greens you ever had in your life!"

serves six to eight

TaG TeAM's SoUthERN gREENs WiTh bACoN

INGREDIENTS

- **8** ounces steak of choice, such as round, skirt, or flank
- **1** teaspoon black pepper
- **2** teaspoons Lawry's seasoned salt (or other meat tenderizer)
- Water (enough to just cover the steak in the pan)
- **1** teaspoon salt

MC BREED MADE IT TO THE BIG TIME THE ROUNDABOUT WAY—from his hometown of Flint, Michigan, he hooked up with an indie record company and struggled until Public Enemy's Chuck D gave him props on "Yo! MTV Raps!" one afternoon and the world began to tune in. *"I cook some of everything, mostly soul food, of course. Smothered steak is the best way, for me. You have to pre-fry it after you season it, and then, while cookin' it, you make your gravy, get you a little flow going, and let it cook for about 40 to 45 minutes."*

"Me myself, I put the steak in the sink, and I take a little pepper—I like spicy food, just not that real peppery hot food—and a little meat tenderizer. Rub it in and then put it in the pot. Then I put some water over it and put some more pepper and a little salt on the meat, give it a little zip taste to it. Cover, cook 40 to 45 minutes until the meat is tender. Serve with rice, gotta have some corn, the creamy corn. Some good Jiffy corn bread, and a big glass of Kool-Aid."

serves two

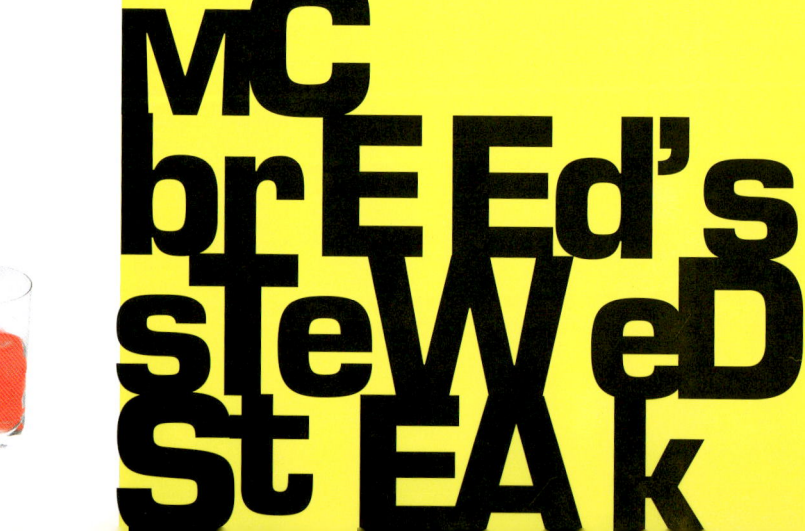

MC brEEd's steWeD stEAk

ON
WAY
21
Or are you thinking
about buying one ?
ELECTRICIAN
"RELIABLE"
AND VERY REASONABLE
(FULLY LICENSED)
"FREE ESTIMATES"

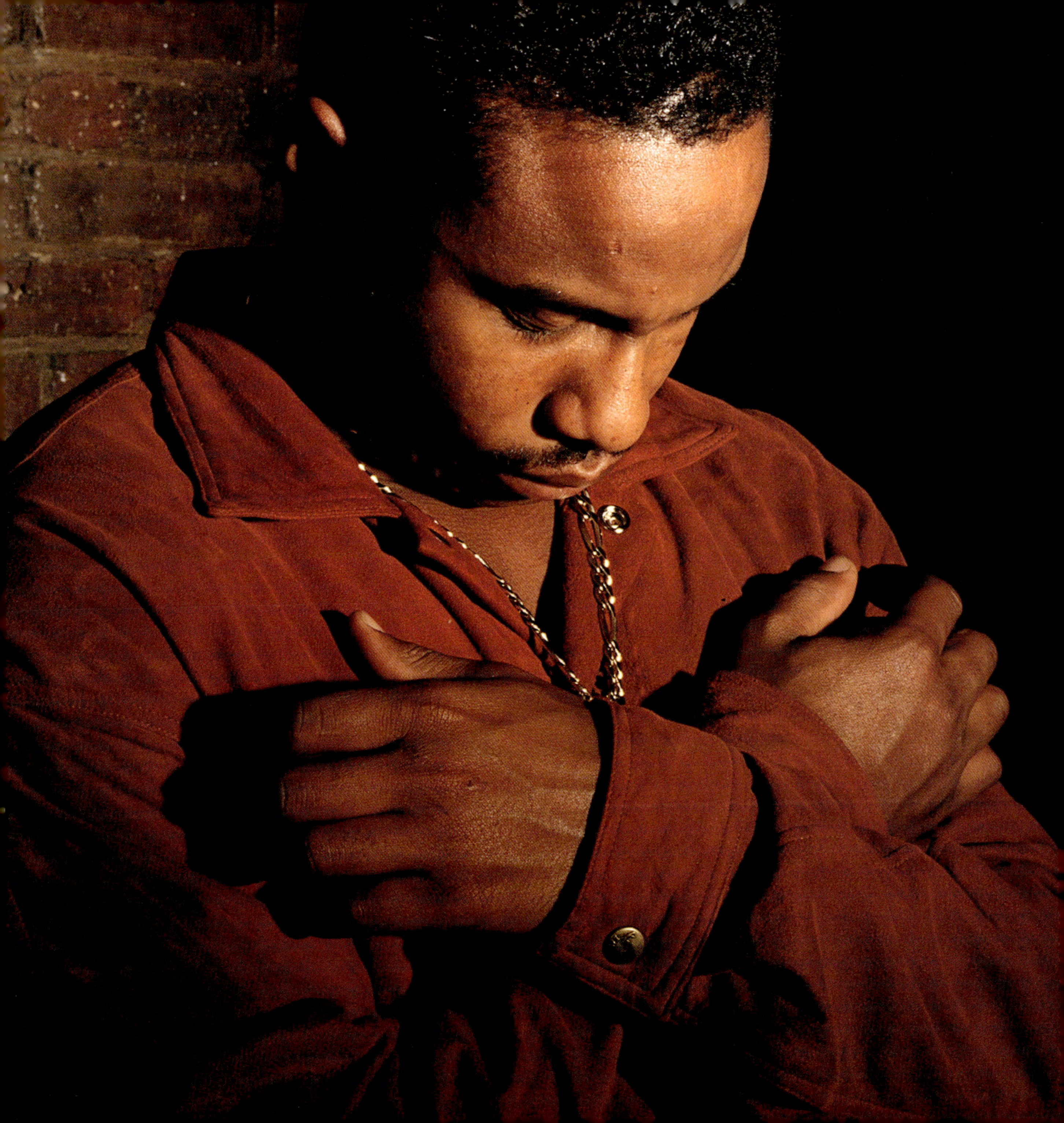

Karl Kani's Turkey Sandwich with Avocado

THE GLAD-RAGS OF THE HIP-HOP WORLD owe an awful lot to Karl Kani's imprint. A leading designer with **Cross Colours**, Kani mixed the street-edge of his Brooklyn coming-of-age with the colorful traditions of his family's heritage (they hail from **Panama** and **Costa Rica**) to create a style all his own. In **1994**, he broke free of his old employer to create his own company. Entrepreneurial spirit notwithstanding, he's got time for a few dalliances. *"Yeah, you know, I cook a lot, play a little Chef-Boy-Ar-Dee business in the kitchen sometimes. I hook up a little baked chicken business, baked chicken and rice, and turkey breast sandwiches with avocado. Sometimes, it ain't good to go out all the time, so you stay home and whip up somethin' real quick. You season it up, throw it in the oven, parlay, drink a brew, and you come back and eat your chicken. The sandwich is even easier."*

"You take your avocado, slice it in half, chop it up real quick. Slam it up—I don't waste no time when I eat! You got to use the dark mustard on this, the spicy business. Got to love that spicy food! And that's it." **serves one**

INGREDIENTS

- 1 avocado
- 2 slices whole wheat bread
- 8 slices turkey breast
- 1 teaspoon mayonnaise
- 1 teaspoon Gulden's mustard, "the dark, spicy one"
- 1 tomato, cored and sliced
- ¼ head lettuce
- 2 slices cheese

"I eat vegetarian now, no meat whatsoever. And I feel a lot healthier because of it, too. My baby, Kiani has never had it. I haven't had beef or pork since she was born. Havin' a baby has made me very conscious of our health."—Dee Barnes

vEgeTabLe s

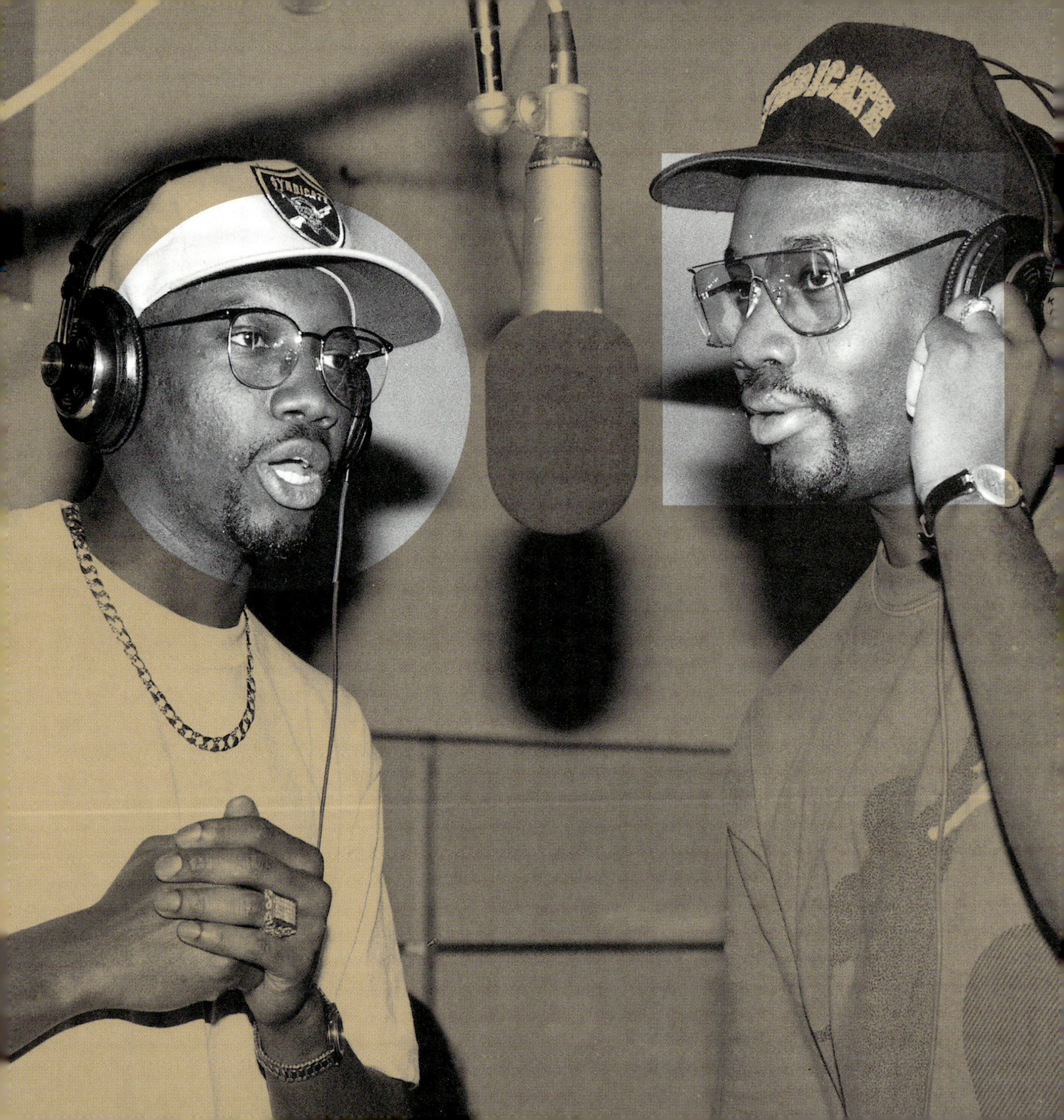

KNOWN MOSTLY FOR TAGGING ALONG with his brother Evil-E on jams with Ice-T, Hen-G still manages to lay down dark and thoughtful work when the two brothers pull together their solo joints. The styles of both coasts color their work in the studio and on the stovetop. "We moved out to LA from New York about 15 years ago, and I've found that the food has so much more flavor in New York. Except Mexican, which is good in LA. My moms does most of the cookin' for us, though, 'cause I got to take care of my music. We eat mostly Honduran food when she cooks, and that's great. The thing I like best when she makes it is plantains. I can make 'em, too!"

"Heat up the oil in the skillet until very hot. Then, chop them plantains up real thin and throw them into the pan until crisp. Sometimes, I like to throw that chicken in there, that really catches the flavor! Me and my brother like it this way!" **serves two**

hEN-g's fRiEd PLANTAINS

INGREDIENTS

- **3** teaspoons vegetable oil
- **2** plantains or large bananas
- **1** cup cooked chicken, chopped (optional)

79

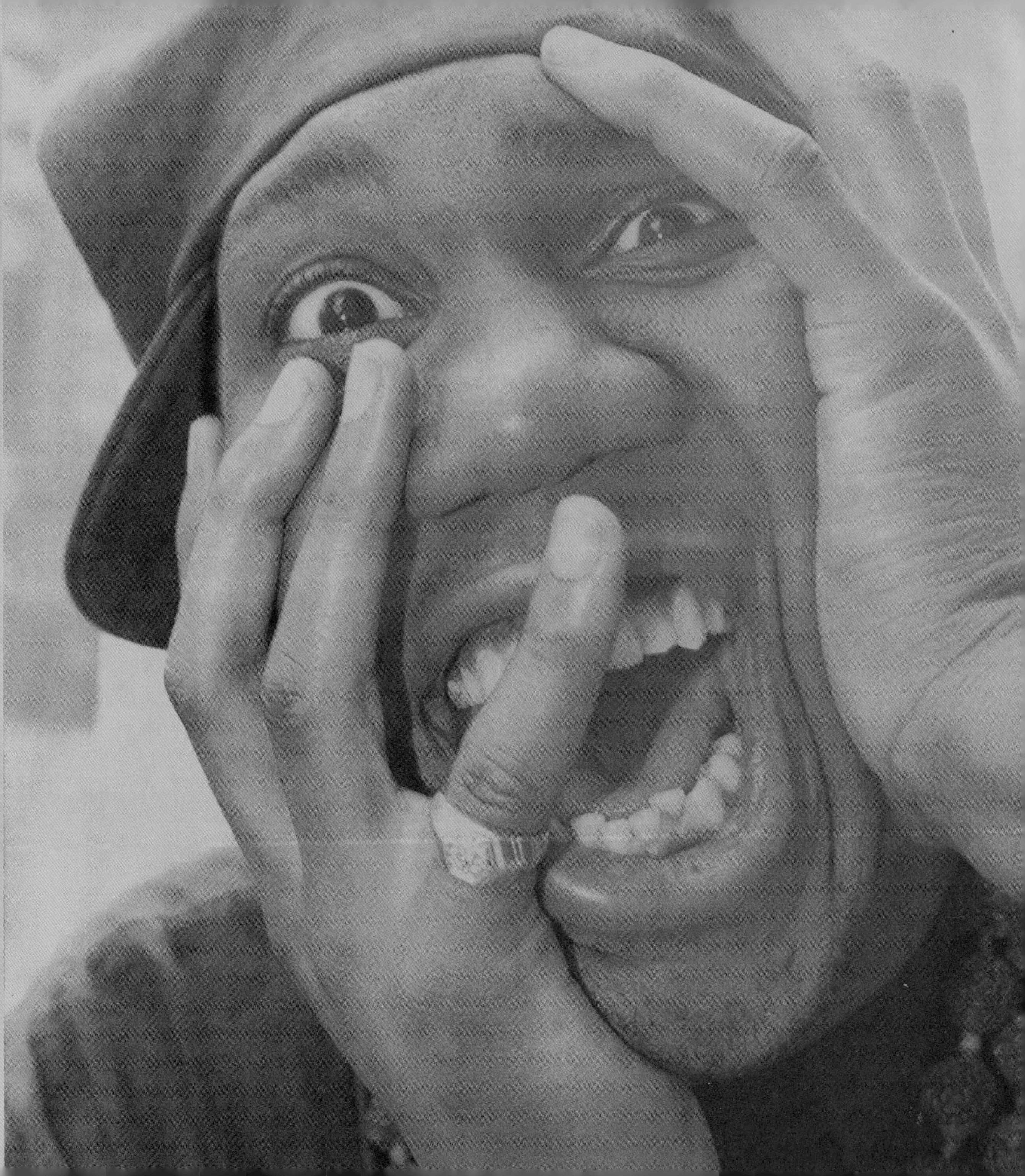

KRS-ONE'S bROCCoLi + cHEESE

KRS-ONE IS ONE OF HIP-HOP'S GREATEST INNOVATORS, and also one of its great expounders. Ask him any question and he'll have a number of viable answers for it. His love of food approximates his love for performing and taking listeners in new directions. *"I'll tell you what I eat: fish. If I can get to a vegetarian place, I'll eat a vegetarian something. Why get a hamburger? They have all of these chicken-flavored vegetarian dishes, which I don't understand. Something in the combination is supposed to trigger 'chicken.' I would have meat if I wanted meat. I prefer boiled foods, and I love broccoli. I don't get to cook much, so I buy Chinese food a lot. I like all the starches. . . .I like rye bread, but you can't get that Pathmark rye bread, it's got to be real rye bread! I also like all sorts of dairy products and soup, and I usually eat peanuts, but they have a lot of fat and are gassy, so lentils are better. The lentil is smaller—20 lentils equals a peanut. One bowl of lentil soup is like three hamburgers in protein! A bowl of soup, some rye bread, some OJ and boom! Your body loves you! If you really want it to love you, eat this with water. If you really really want it to love you, go for a walk afterwards."*

INGREDIENTS

- 3-4 heads broccoli, tough stems removed
- 8 ounces American cheese

"Take three or four heads of broccoli, and steam or cook in one pot, while melting the cheese in another. The Welfare cheese was the hypest cheese, but I can't get it anywhere now! After about 7 minutes, remove the broccoli, pour the cheese over it and have some rye bread with it. That alone is a full, excellent meal." **serves two**

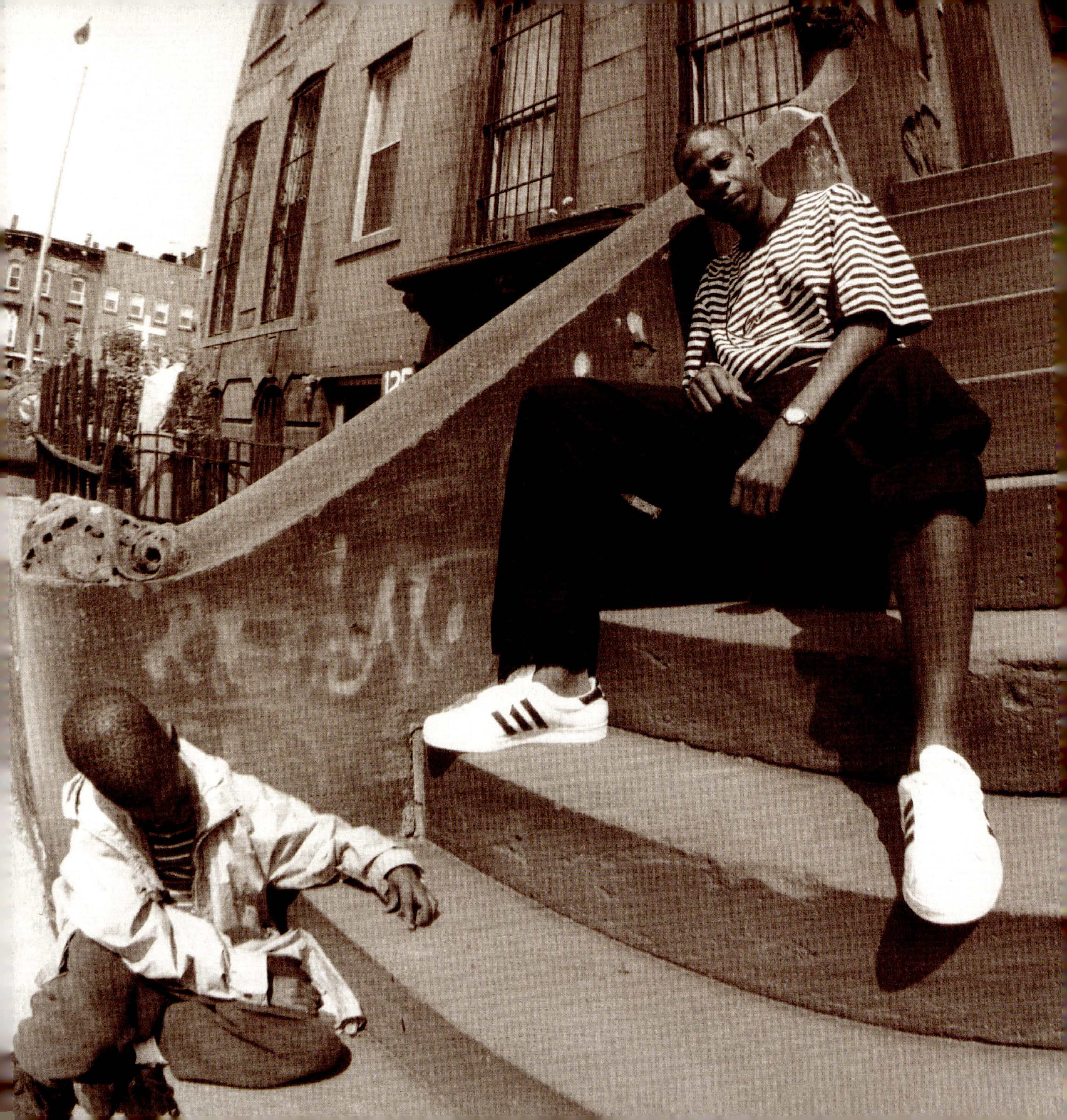

dOUg E. fReSH's bARbEcUEd POTaToES

DOUG E. FRESH FIRST CRASHED THE HIP-HOP SCENE in the mid-80s with one of the all-time killer party records, *The Show*. His good-natured mix of Old-School sensibility and youthful exuberance instantly made him a favorite with fans, and his "human beat box" moves made him a standout in the movie *Tapeheads*. "I like to cook, and I like to make original dishes. I know how to make most regular dishes, too. I got this stuff I make called 'Barbecued Potatoes.' A friend of mine called Stretch likes it. He did the choreography for Michael Jackson's video, so he must know something."

"Barbecued potatoes is the thing he likes because I take the potatoes [peel and chop into chunks] and I put them in pepper and vegetable salt and let them sit there [approximately 10 minutes]. Then, I chop up the cheddar cheese real fine. I use the garlic, onion, and barbecue sauce and I let it soak up in there, along with the margarine. It's like cookin' 'em like home fries. I mix in the peppers and I use lemon pepper instead of salt 'cause it's like salt, only you don't have to have the salt. You heat it all up for 45 to 55 minutes in the covered skillet on medium heat and it's ready. It's mean! It's mean!" **serves four to six**

INGREDIENTS

- 3-4 Idaho potatoes,
- 2 tablespoons lemon pepper
- 2 tablespoons vegetable salt
- 1/2 pound cheddar cheese
- 1 clove garlic, finely chopped
- 1 onion, chopped
- 1 cup barbecue sauce
- 1/2 cup margarine, melted
- 1/2 red pepper, cored, seeded, and chopped
- 1 green pepper, cored, seeded, and chopped

Angie Stone's Slammin' Yams

ANGIE STONE IS ONE OF RAP'S PLEASANT LITTLE SECRETS. She began plying her trade back in the first days of vinyl, rolling with the Sugar Hill Records mob. Times, and Angie herself, have changed, and nowadays she tosses the hip-hop element into her work as part of the New York trio Vertical Hold. *"I cook collard greens, of course chicken, I love cookin' steak and they love my yams! I make 'em with real butter, cinnamon, nutmeg, and lemon peels. I just take the lemon peel and lay it over the top, so that the juices from the lemon peel go into the potato."*

Preheat the oven to 350°F. "What I do is, I dice the yams. I slice 'em and dice 'em. I then put the water in the bottom of the skillet, 'cause you know potatoes make their own water. And you can cook 'em on the stovetop, but if you cook 'em in the oven and steam 'em, and put that butter and spices and maybe a little sugar in there; it melts down and kinda sautés them. And then you can put a drop of vanilla in there and drive 'em crazy! If you use a baking dish and do them in the oven, cook them for about 45 minutes, depending on how thick you slice 'em. They can break down a little, but that's all the more better 'cause then they melt in your mouth!" **serves two**

INGREDIENTS

- 2 large yams, peeled, sliced in small wedges
- 1/3 cup water
- 1 tablespoon butter
- 1/2 teaspoon ground nutmeg
- 1/2 teaspoon ground cinnamon
- 1 tablespoon brown sugar (optional)
- 1 teaspoon vanilla extract

JAMAL-SKI SLID INTO RAP UNDER THE COVER OF KRS-ONE'S UMBRELLA group, Boogie Down Productions. Now he's spreading his reggae-rap solo and also makin' noise with the pots and pans. *"I could give it to you in the chat, but so I'll be legible, I gonna tell you—the only time I eat any good food is when I cook, I cook for myself. I also live with two people who are straight up holistic, not like myself, because I have certain bad habits."*

"Heat up the oil. Always ginger, onions, and garlic as your foundation elements. Then we use noodles, first boil them, drain well, and then fry them in the skillet. Add the tofu—I'm down with soy milk, 100%! Cook the onion, ginger, and garlic in the skillet, and add a little tamari. You can add tamari after, too, but it's good to cook in with the other vegetables and tofu. Then, you just fry the tofu until it's brown and crispy, so it doesn't taste wack! Most people are like, 'Oh, tofu!' but if you do it right, the shit is on!" serves three

jAMAl-sKi's toFU stIr-fRY

INGREDIENTS

1/3 cup sesame oil
1 piece ginger, peeled and chopped
1 onion, chopped
1 clove garlic, finely chopped
6 ounces noodles
3 inch block of tofu, sliced, "you can buy loose pieces, but I slice 'em down, break 'em down"
Dash tamari or soy sauce
1 cup broccoli, cut into small pieces
1 carrot, cut into small pieces

QUICK
BITES

"I don't cook too much. It's carrot sticks for me! I used to cook. When I get older and slow down, I'm gettin' in that kitchen again. I used to make cakes and pastries, more baking than anything. Just cakes—vanilla cakes with chocolate frosting. Yeah, I'm gonna be fat at the end of my thing. I'm gonna be a round, little butterball!"—Vinny (Naughty By Nature)

dEssErts

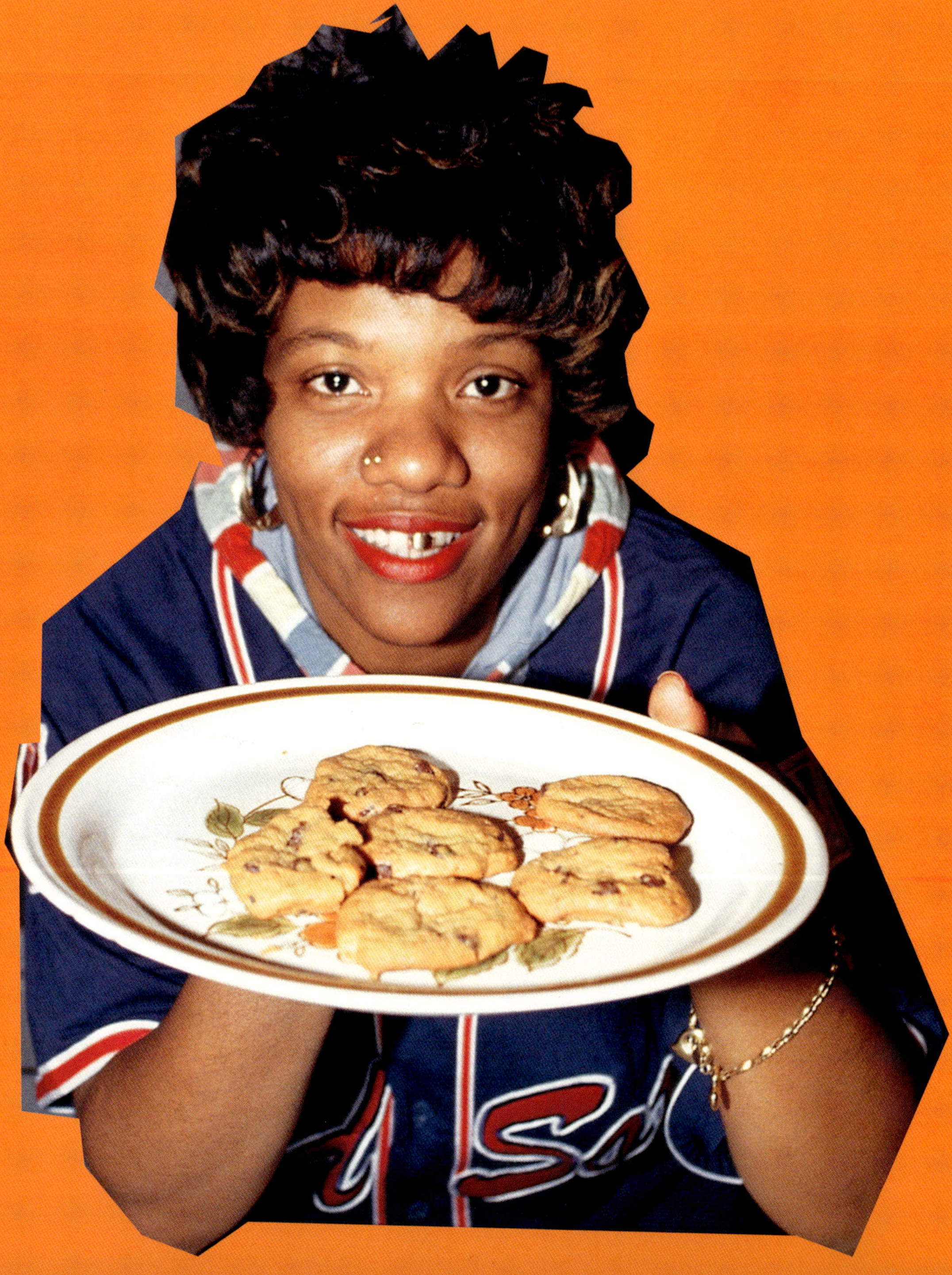

INGREDIENTS

1 cup all-purpose flour
½ teaspoon baking soda
½ teaspoon salt
¾ cup butter, softened
6 tablespoons granulated sugar
6 tablespoons brown sugar, firmly packed
½ teaspoon vanilla extract
1 large egg
6 ounces semi-sweet chocolate morsels

nIKKI D's CHoCoLATE CHiP CooKiEs

BESIDES WORKING BOTH SIDES OF HER RECORDS now (recording as well as managing at Def Jam), Nikki D is an accomplished chef. *"I try to cook whatever I can before I leave for the studio. This way I've got something good to eat when I'm coming home late at night."*

Preheat the oven to 375°F. "Mix the flour, baking soda, and salt in one bowl. In another, mix butter, both of the sugars, and vanilla until they are creamy. Then, add the egg. Slowly add to the other bowl and add the morsels. Drop by the spoonful on an ungreased cookie sheet and bake for 9 to 11 minutes, then repeat. Enjoy!"

yields 20 to 24 cookies, or enough for the posse

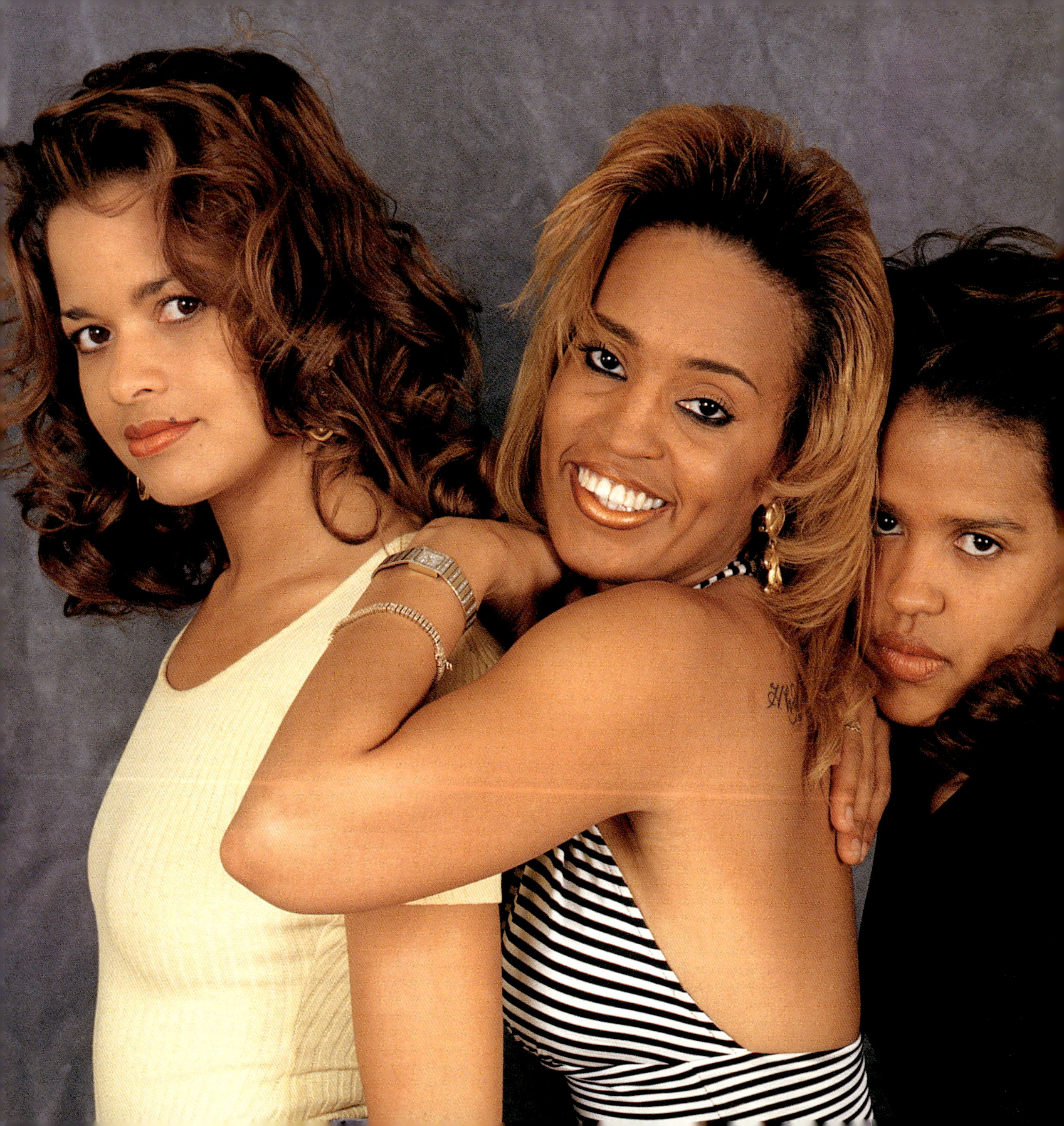

H.W.A. (Hoes With aTTiTudE)'s sweet potato pie

EVERYBODY'S FAVORITE HOES live by Robert Townshend's edict—"Hoes got to eat, too!" But there were some lean years after their exodus from Chicago. **"We miss White Castle in LA,"** Kim says with a sigh. **"When we moved to LA, we didn't have a White Castle, so we lived off Oodles of Noodles. Everyone's into the health thing in California. We're not. We eat! All three of us live together. Matter of fact, that was the name of our first album, 'Livin' In A Hoe House.' Somebody thought we lived in a boat, we don't. I'm the main cook for us. They like the beans, the turkey, and the sweet potato pie."**

Preheat the oven to 400°F. Mash the potatoes in a mixing bowl. Combine the eggs, sugar, salt, cinnamon, and milk in another bowl. Pour this mixture into the potatoes and "whip it up really, really, really good, and that's all I'm gonna tell you—I put some hoe touch on it after that and it's sooooo good! (Mix in the butter. Pour into the pie crust.) Bake it 'til it browns (45 to 55 minutes, or until the filling is set). We use a lot of ice cream on it, a lot of whipped cream. We use whipped cream on everything. Everything! It's a whipped cream kinda house. Maybe we'll get a whipped cream endorsement soon. We definitely believe in it—you can cream with the hoes!" **serves six to eight**

INGREDIENTS

- 4 medium-size sweet potatoes, cooked until soft and peeled
- 3 eggs, lightly beaten
- 1/3 cup granulated sugar
- 1/4 teaspoon salt
- 3/4 teaspoon ground cinnamon
- 1 16-ounce can Pet condensed milk
- 4 tablespoons unsalted butter, softened
- 1 9-inch ready-made pie crust

QUiCK
BiTES

"Yeah, I like to cook. I cook turkey, chicken, and fish. I don't eat red meat, nor pork. I love rice, and vegetables. I make a lot of salmon croquets and I love chocolate chip cookies—but I'm a fool for cranberry juice, it's my favorite thing."—Nefretiti

BEVERAGES

dOuG E. FrESH's JUmp-Up JUice

ANOTHER HIT FROM NEW YORK'S OWN. "Y'know, I like to make drinks like juices, mix 'em up different. Strawberry, apple, lemon—all in the same drink. I make it in quantity, so when I'm thirsty, I can just go in there and hit it! I don't make one glass at a time 'cause cleanin' up after juicing is the worst thing. I also make energy juices—take carrots, cucumbers, beets, cut the seeds out of the cucumber, juice it, juice the carrots and juice the beets, and when you mix it, it's a real energy booster because the beets stimulate red blood cells. Then you are charged! You gotta use a lot of carrots 'cause the carrots don't give you too much juice. But this other juice, that's my thing, man."

"All you gotta do is mix it up in the blender, nice and smooth, and you've got a great drink. The lemons will keep it fresh longer, too. Yeah, it's good. Real good!" **serves eight**

INGREDIENTS

1	quart strawberries, hulled
10-12	small apples, peeled and cored
	Juice of 2-3 lemons

AND. . . Big Al's hip-hop watering hole faves: Tropicana Twister, Carrot and Apple Juice, Cherry Coke, Peach Snapple, and Slurpies.

INDEX

ANGIE STONE's
  Slammin' Yams, 84
BUSHWICK BILL's
  Bad-boy Wings, 60
CHUBB ROCK's
  Spaghetti à la Chubbs, 27
DOUG E. FRESH's
  Barbecued Potatoes, 83
DOUG E. FRESH's
  Jump-Up Juice, 95
ERICK SERMON's
  Fettucini + Shrimp, 47
FLAVOR-FLAV's
  PE Rice Pilaf, 23
FREEDOM WILLIAMS'
  Stir-fry Lasagna, 31
HARMONY's
  Broiled Bluefish, 43
HEAVY D's
  Lemon Chicken, 55
HEN-G's
  Fried Plantains, 79
H.W.A.'s (Hoes with Attitude)'s
  Sweet Potato Pie, 91
IMMATURE's
  Quick Chicken Stir-fry, 69
INNER SOUL's
  French Kiss Toast, 17
JAMAL-SKI's
  Tofu Stir-fry, 85
JAZZY JOYCE's
  Pasta with Shrimp, 24
JUST-ICE's
  Hot Curried Goat, 63
KARL KANI's
  Turkey Sandwich with Avocado, 75
KID CAPRI's
  Shrimps Parmesan, 48
KID 'N PLAY's
  Hard Luck Franks 'n Beans, 59
KOOL MOE DEE's
  Shrimp Scampi, 39

K-ROCK's
  Breakfast Grits, 34
KRS-ONE's
  Broccoli + Cheese, 81
MARLEY MARL's
  Fried Chicken, 64
MC BREED's
  Stewed Steak, 72
MC LYTE's
  Devilish Deviled Eggs, 13
MIKE G's
  JB Salmon Cakes, 49
MONIE LOVE's
  Incredible Chicken Curry, 67
MS. MELODIE's
  Sizzlin' Stewfish, 40
NIKKI D's
  Chocolate Chip Cookies, 89
QUEEN LATIFAH's
  Royal Turkey Cutlets, 57
RAMPAGE's
  Simple Scrambled Eggs + Cheese, 1
RESIDENT ALIEN's
  Rice, Peas + Coconut, 28
ROSIE PEREZ's
  Really Rosie Red Sauce, 35
ROXANNE's
  Baked Ziti, Boriqua-style, 32
ROXANNE'S MOM's
  Sofrito, 33
SPIN's
  Spaghettirella, 25
TAG TEAM's
  Fried Pork Chops, Southern Style, 70
TAG TEAM's
  Southern Greens with Bacon, 71
TIM DOG's
  Rabid Red Rice, 20
YOUNG MC's
  Vegetable + Pasta Medley, 29
YO-YO's
  Burritos à la Yo-Yo, 53
ZIGGY MARLEY's
  Snapper Delight, 44